More Praise for *Riding the Tiger*

"I'm a huge fan of actionable checklists; they work. This book not only explains what to do for organizations in serious crisis, but the principles are equally valuable for every business in good times and bad times."

Jack Zenger
CEO, Zenger|Folkman
Co-author of the bestselling *The Extraordinary Leader*
and *The Inspiring Leader*

"To be faced with a crisis the magnitude of what Satyam dealt with and then one year later to be reborn and vibrant in a new avatar speaks volumes about the value of a strong leadership culture. This resilience is the result of years of painstakingly implemented leadership development strategies, which were spearheaded by teams led by Ed Cohen and in which Priscilla Nelson was also a highly influential senior leader. As a beneficiary of the leadership techniques covered in this book, I believe they are a must for all who aspire to succeed in today's world."

Venkatesh Roddam
Director, VenSat Tech India
Former CEO at Satyam BPO

"Rarely does a book come along that is as useful as *Riding the Tiger*. Ed and Priscilla have turned their turbulent experiences into a realistic how-to guide for the rest of us. They show how to move from crisis to credibility of leadership; from pain to passion for the brand; and from scandal to renewed success. Using their practical experiences as a basis, they share action item lists, introduce a new vocabulary, suggest questions to ask, and present a plan to move boldly forward from chaos to confidence. This is not a book to be read, but one to put into action, especially when you are riding your own tiger."

Elaine Biech
Author of *The Business of Consulting* and *Thriving Through Change*

"*Riding the Tiger* is a unique book, and Ed and Priscilla are the perfect people to write it. Two authors with a life-long dedication to leadership and learning used all of their experience and skills to meet the ultimate business challenge. It's a very exciting read with hundreds of practical tips."

Marty Seldman, Ph.D.
Author of *Executive Stamina*
Author of *Wall Street Journal* bestseller *Survival of the Savvy*

"*Riding the Tiger* is a terrific read for any leader who is challenged to navigate her organization through a time of turbulence. In the new age of the anti-heroes in this economy, Priscilla Nelson and Ed Cohen provide sensitive insight and give practical steps to regain hope for the future. They are among the most inspiring leaders I've met. When you read this book, you will walk in the perceptive footsteps of remarkable leaders who help define tomorrow's business."

Barbara Singer Cheng
President & CEO
Executive Core

"I have had the privilege of working with Ed Cohen at Booz Allen Hamilton and both Ed and Priscilla at Satyam. They put tremendous energy, passion, and talent into learning and development. *Riding the Tiger* details their use of leading through learning at a point of crisis in Satyam. I recommend the lessons from this book not only for handling crisis in a corporation, but more importantly, handling the changes that all corporations have to deal with every year."

Bill Thoet
Senior Vice President
Booz Allen Hamilton

"While many books focus on successful organizations and winning moves, *Riding the Tiger* is a refreshing and masterful piece of work that distills lessons from the traumatic fall of a great enterprise. Few people in the world have propounded on leadership and organizational improvement in a compelling and systematic way as Priscilla Nelson and Ed Cohen."

Tan Yinglan
Author
The Way Of The VC: Top Venture Capitalists On Your Board

"While presented in the context of extreme crisis, the insights and advice that Priscilla Nelson and Ed Cohen share are widely applicable. Accordingly, *Riding the Tiger* is a valuable resource for any leader looking to be equally prepared for both unforeseen catastrophes as well as everyday hurdles."

Michael Rosenthal
CEO
Consensus Group

"A smooth sea never makes a good sailor. Turbulence is essential to build character and strengthen resolve. Every organization and individual will have their moments of riding the tiger. Leading with a clear focus and with integrity is essential to adequately manage these choppy times. Reading this book was enriching, educating, and entertaining. A must-read for every business leader."

Mukesh Aghi Ph.D.
Chairman & CEO
Steria India

Riding the Tiger

Riding the Tiger

Leading Through Learning
in Turbulent Times

Priscilla Nelson
Ed Cohen

ASTD
PRESS

Alexandria, Virginia

ASTD Press is an internationally renowned source of insightful and practical information on workplace learning and performance topics, including training basics, evaluation and return-on-investment, instructional systems development, e-learning, leadership, and career development. Visit us at www.astd.org/astdpress.

Ordering information: Books published by ASTD Press can be purchased by visiting ASTD's website at store.astd.org or by calling 800.628.2783 or 703.683.8100.

Library of Congress Control Number: 2009939714

ISBN-10: 1-56286-734-2
ISBN-13: 978-1-56286-734-8

ASTD Press Editorial Staff:

Director of Content: Adam Chesler
Manager, ASTD Press: Jacqueline Edlund-Braun
Senior Associate Editor: Tora Estep
Senior Associate Editor: Justin Brusino
Editorial Assistant: Victoria DeVaux

Copyeditor: Alfred Imhoff
Indexing and Proofreading: Abella Publishing Services, LLC
Interior Design: Kathleen Schaner
Interior Production: PerfecType, Nashville, TN
Cover Design: Ana Ilieva Foreman
Cover Art: Getty Images
Frontispiece Illustration: Jennifer Haefeli

Printed by United Book Press, Inc., Baltimore, Maryland

We dedicate this book to the tens of thousands of Satyam employees and their families, suppliers, customers, and investors who with us experienced Satyam's turbulent journey—what was, what could have been, and what is yet to be seen.

Contents

Foreword

It is rare in life that you experience events so profound that they become memory markers. My brief time working with Satyam Computer Services and being introduced to India was one of those events. Most who visit India for the first time note the never-ending stream of dichotomies they encounter—wealth/poverty, beauty/squalor, hospitality/violence, creative energy/desperation. My experience with Satyam followed in kind.

As a business leader and learning professional, my eye is always geared toward exploring insights into learning cultures and models. During my visit to India in 2008, I was the keynote speaker for the Indian Society for Training & Development's annual conference, which was hosted by Satyam. I was immediately struck by the power of Satyam's image and infrastructure. The support provided for the conference in the sparkling, high-technology facility in Hyderabad was impressive. Even more affecting was the learning culture that had been created by Ed Cohen and Priscilla Nelson. A few days later, I facilitated an offsite seminar for Satyam professionals on how they could use a "whole brain" approach in designing their teaching and learning. I had the unique opportunity to discover Satyam via this vibrant, growing team of professionals, who demonstrated such passion and dedication to their mission that, at first, I was a bit suspicious. As my time with them unfolded, however, I felt the power of an organizational culture that was designed on the basis of learning and growth—in contrast to so many, who treat learning as a separate function or an add-on. The leadership approach that Ed and Priscilla delineated at this seminar has as one of its core principles the recognition that a learning organization is engendered from within each employee and the infrastructure that is made available to them.

This brief remembrance cannot possibly do justice to the power and impact these few days at Satyam had on me. It pales in comparison with the impact that Satyam's learning organization had for the thousands that it touched through the good times and even as the consequences of the debacle that later unfolded at Satyam. I left India with hope in my heart that other organizations like Satyam existed in India and could provide the learning opportunities that so few other enterprises ever consider. Months later, seeing the Satyam team receive its Excellence in Practice award at the meeting of the American Society for Training & Development made the memory even sweeter.

The sudden news of Satyam's crisis had an equal impact and brought forth one more dichotomy: success/fraud. How could this reversal be possible? As I learned more, I tried to find consolation in the sense of hope with which I had left India. My heart ached for the thousands of people who were not only losing their jobs but were also seething with a sense of personal and professional betrayal that most of us could never come close to knowing. As with many of these tragedies, there were no easy answers or antidotes. Struggling with my own disbelief and outrage, I prayed that the gift of hope would endure.

Brain research shows us that memory markers exist because the emotional impact of certain events embed these experiences in long-term memory. In this respect, I knew that thousands had been touched by the power of the excellent learning culture at Satyam, which they would carry with them forever. That could never be taken from them. My wishes are that there is enough hope left to combat the easy pessimism that accompanies the harsh reality of the consequences faced by those in power and that lessons are learned from this tragic story.

This book will provide you with the hope and many lessons learned from the experiences of Satyam and other organizations of all kinds around the world that have been helped by Ed Cohen and Priscilla Nelson. You'll receive fantastic insights and practical guidelines that can be implemented by leaders in any organization facing turmoil—and these days that includes most of us. The turmoil could be a result of significant change or lack of change; of rapid growth or rapid decline; of a merger, acquisition, or takeover; or of key leaders joining or leaving. It may be more extreme, resulting from a calamity such as a financial scandal or the theft of intellectual property, or an unnatural (terrorist attack) or natural (earthquake, monsoon) disaster affecting any part of the organization. In the pages that follow, Priscilla and Ed share their lessons—along with the lessons learned by all the leaders and employees of Satyam who struggled to pick up the shattered pieces and rebuild the company as they recovered from their crisis.

Riding the Tiger: Leading Through Learning in Turbulent Times does not dwell on Satyam's crisis or how it occurred. Instead, Priscilla and Ed take you on a journey to discover how the process and steps of "leading through learning" were discovered and engaged, providing powerful insights and guidelines to illuminate the path of understanding and development for leaders faced with guiding their organizations through any kind of crisis.

As you read this book, you will be encouraged to consider all the ways you will be able to apply its practical guidelines and advice to calm the chaos in your organization—making way for new creative energy, enhanced passion, and great success.

Ann Herrmann-Nehdi
CEO, Herrmann International, publisher of the
Herrmann Brain Dominance Instrument

Preface

✦ ✦ ✦

It was like riding a tiger, not knowing how to get off without being eaten.

—Ramalinga Raju

✦ ✦ ✦

This quote is how Ramalinga Raju, the founder and chairman of Satyam Computer Services, based in Hyderabad, described the widening gap between the real and artificial numbers in the company's books when he confessed to the actions that caused Satyam's fall from grace on January 7, 2009. Satyam, which was founded in 1987, had grown to be the fourth largest information technology services firm in India, with more than 53,000 employees working in 60 countries around the world. But now the adjectives used to refer to this once-iconic brand, whose slogan had been "India is IT," were tainted, disgraced, beleaguered, scandalized, fraudulent, and crisis-ridden. The huge scale and impact of Satyam's downfall were clear in the headline of *The Economist*'s cover story: "India's Enron," and *Business-Week* featured a photo of Raju on the cover with the headline "From Icon to I Con."

Even in the maelstrom of this scandal, however, for the vast majority of Satyam's dedicated leaders, daily life at the firm still came first—customer retention, revenue, collections, delivery of projects, and tending to wounded employees. Yet Satyam's leaders, and in fact most leaders in India, had never encountered anything like this. Employee morale had plummeted to an instant all-time low, no one knew whom to trust, and feelings of betrayal had left a sour aftertaste.

But this book does not tell the story of Satyam's downfall. It tells about what happened after Raju's confession and how a "leading through learning" strategy was implemented to stabilize the company and help it recover and rebuild. Moreover, though the story of the crisis endured by Satyam's leaders and employees in Hyderabad is engrossing, the leadership lessons from their experiences are just as applicable to a nonprofit advocacy organization in Baltimore, an agricultural products firm in Omaha, a sporting goods retailer in Beijing, an investment bank in Sydney, or a high-technology firm in San Jose. These lessons, in short, are universal; whenever people in an organization are facing turbulence—whether caused by external recession, internal malfeasance, or anything else—the organization's leaders and all employees' efforts to continue essential initiatives play a key role in resolving issues and putting the organization back on an even keel. Thus, when a crisis hits and the going gets *beyond* tough, when it gets nearly impossible, this crisis itself—in accord with the Chinese proverb—is paradoxically both a grave danger and a great opportunity to set the organization on a path toward renewal.

This book gives you a specific, step-by-step approach to this organizational renewal spurred by leading through learning. After chapter 1 introduces you to the cast of characters and main themes, chapter 2 shows you how to use an essential tool we've developed based on our lessons from Satyam's experience (and those of many other organizations we've assisted over the years): the "Lights On" strategy—a vital first step for a business in crisis, which simply is to keep the lights on and do only what's absolutely necessary to stabilize operations and regain forward momentum. Chapters 3 and 4 offer detailed practical steps and guidelines for leading through learning in turbulent times. Then several chapters cover essential aspects of this leadership and its related functions—coaching in chapter 5, maximizing the value of social networking media in chapter 6, caring for those wounded by a crisis in chapter 7, and responding to customers in real time in chapter 8. Finally, chapter 9 distills the specifics of the earlier chapters to enable you to create a postcrisis, longer-term plan for growth. Throughout all these chapters, you will find fascinating, pointed stories about people who've utilized the tools we're describing, and wise quotations illuminating the principles underlying these techniques. Two appendixes are full of even more provocative, inspiring lessons and stories from the Satyam experience.

So now, without further ado, we invite you to take that tiger by the tail so you won't be eaten and learn how to actually enjoy the challenge of leading your organization through learning to survive and thrive during what you may have feared were impossibly chaotic times.

Acknowledgments

From the start of Satyam's crisis, we knew there would be many lessons, even painful ones, that would prove valuable for business professionals around the world. And so we embarked on our journey. Knowing that we will most likely and inadvertently forget to thank a few people, we first offer our appreciation to all our colleagues, friends, and family who provided input, guidance, and support. With that caveat, we are especially grateful to everyone at ASTD Press for all their efforts to make this book happen within a very compressed timeline, including Dean Smith, who developed an outstanding partnership with us; Justin Brusino, who provided encouragement and edits; Alfred Imhoff, our copyeditor; and Jacqueline Edlund-Braun, who managed the entire process. And thanks to Tony Bingham, the president of ASTD, who supported our desire to share our journey of leading through learning with the world.

We are thankful to all the contributors to the book. Ann Herrmann-Nehdi came to India and introduced "whole brain thinking" to the learning profession and wrote our wonderful foreword. Emily King inspired the four steps for change discussed in chapter 4. Arunav Sinha co-authored the section on moving up the relationship chain in chapter 7. Vandana Jayakumar and Nagendra V. Chowdary wrote and provided permission to use the Satyam case study, which is available at our website for this book (ridingthetiger.com). Michael Cramer provided an overview of social networking. Joshua Craver and Sai Gollapudi contributed to the design of real-time learning and the leadership audit. Anil Santhapuri documented lessons learned from the *Rise of the Phoenix* web TV show (see chapter 6) and shared his feelings in appendix B. Our profound thanks also go to our other contributors, each of whom continues to inspire us: Rahul Andrews, Dinesh Neelakandan, Tony Chapman, Joshua Craver, Nandini Darsi, Sanjay Devudu, Hetzel Folden, Kishore Goud, Sirisha Kommireddi, Ramesh Kuttappan, David Levitt, Ethan Avadh Levitt, Nishi Levitt, Bhaskar Natarajan, Joydeb Pal, Sita Pallacholla, Pragnya Seth, Rohan Shahane, Venkata Subender, Chrysosthenis Taslis, and Archana Vyasam. And we give special thanks to our early readers, Nicola Klein, Pragnya Seth, and Cheri Torres.

Other special people who inspired and guided us include (but are not limited to) B. Prashanth, for his positive outlook on life, who at the age of 11 years has been through more than most people endure in a lifetime; John P. Kotter, for inspiring change and being a mentor from afar; Beverly Kaye, for being our guru on people; and A.S. Murthy, for leading with heart. And we would be remiss not to mention our appreciation for the efforts of the Indian government officials who assisted Satyam during its crisis and appointed a new board of directors; and to Anand Mahindra and Vineet Nayyar, the Tech Mahindra leaders who demonstrated empathy and truthfulness upon acquiring Satyam.

We are thankful for the efforts and guidance provided by Hari Ankem and the UV Communications team; to Barbara Singer Cheng, for showing empathy and understanding on the journey; to Vijay Gupta and Kameshwari Phani, for assisting us as we maneuvered through the system to repatriate back to the United States; and to Sunita and Natraj, for sharing their lives with us, for including us in their marriage ceremony, and for requesting that we be present for the birth of Shreyas.

Our heartfelt appreciation goes to Elana Cohen and Howard Richmond for providing constant, unconditional love, support, and encouragement along the tumultuous pathway.

We are thankful to Jennifer Haefeli, a wonderful artist and daughter, who painted the white tiger used inside the book; the original hangs on a wall in our home.

And we are eternally grateful to our daughter, MacKenzie Cohen, who demonstrated maturity throughout her senior year of high school in India as we endured all the changes resulting from the Satyam debacle.

We stand in appreciation.

Priscilla Nelson and Ed Cohen

Organizational Crisis Strikes: The Legacy of the Satyam Experience

On January 7, 2009, Ramalinga Raju, the founder and chairman of Satyam Computer Services, disclosed the actions that would cause the company's fall from grace. Those of us who were shareholders saw our investments disappear like a tsunami into a pool of financial destruction. We all looked on in disbelief as the news emerged (figure 1-1). It was 11 a.m. in Hyderabad. Up to that moment, we had all been immersed in planning and delivering learning.

I—Priscilla—was the global director of people leadership at Satyam. As part of the company's overall leadership for learning, I had responsibility for helping leaders better manage their teams and enhance relationships to achieve greater retention of both staff and customers as well as business success. That morning, I had dropped MacKenzie, our daughter, off at the international high school. It was the start of her final semester, and she was very excited. We had returned to India from our holiday in the United States early so she could start on time. My husband, Ed, who was chief learning officer for Satyam, had stayed behind in the San Diego area for a few extra days in our new home.

1

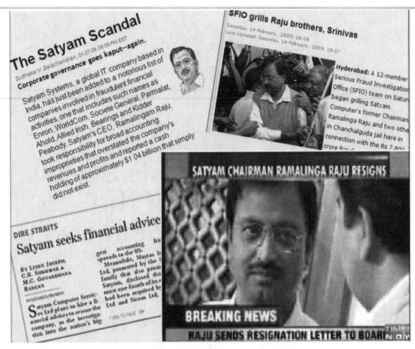

Figure 1-1. *The Satyam Scandal Was Front-Page News for Months. (Image credits: upper-left image, Balachandran, 2009; upper-right image, Joseph, Sukumar, and Rangan, 2009; lower-left image, Sify Business, 2009; lower-right image, News Now, 2009.)*

There we were, close to 50 of us huddled in a small conference room, watching the television, shocked beyond belief. The screen displayed a photo of Raju on the right and a graph depicting the falling stock price on the left. The value of our stock had plummeted in less than 5 seconds, drained like an hourglass. I immediately grabbed my phone and called Ed. He did not answer. It rang and rang. I tried the home phone, and no one answered there either. I continued to call every few minutes (see Voice of Ed Cohen in Appendix B).

The reporter on TV began reading a letter from Raju: "It is with deep regret, and tremendous burden that I am carrying on my conscience, that I would like to bring the following facts to your notice." We watched in disbelief as the news emerged. The letter indicated that for the most recent quarter ending September 2008, Satyam's bank balances had been overstated by close to $81 million and more than $265 million in liabilities were not accounted for.

How could this be true? Just last week, there had been an article in the newspaper indicating that Satyam had an excess of $1.6 billion in cash. The reporter continued: "The gap in the balance sheet has arisen purely on account of inflated profits over a period of the last several years. What started as a marginal gap between actual operating profit and the one reflected in the books of accounts continued to grow over the years."

We later found out that this deception had been going on since 2001 and that it added up to more than $2.5 billion. Everything we had created at Satyam—our Taj Mahal of learning (see appendix A)—was starting to crack and crumble.

"Every attempt made to eliminate the gap failed," Raju's letter continued. "As the promoters held a small percentage of equity, the concern was that poor performance would result in takeover, thereby exposing the gap. It was like riding a tiger, not knowing how to get off without being eaten."

What had we missed? The unthinkable was playing out before our eyes. Could this all be true? I had actually been worried about Raju for months. His recent lack of communication was a red flag. I had spent years as a psychotherapist and worried that the economic fallout now reaching India was taking its toll. I'd even tried to speak with him, and he had quickly changed the subject and darted off to another meeting. Ed also sent a note to Raju indicating that people were starting to worry and needed some form of communication from him. He finally sent out a brief note saying that it was concerning for us all to watch the economy affect us, yet we were prepared and had enough to "weather it." He asked for everyone's support, and we had all willingly given it.

Now his letter ended: "Under the circumstances, I am tendering my resignation as the chairman of Satyam and shall continue in this position only till such time as the current board is expanded."

We were numb. None of us believed that Raju could have such a dark side. We all worried that without him—our founder, our leader, the man who defined Satyam—the company would not survive. But we wondered who he really was (see the sidebar, and for a more detailed account of what happened at Satyam, including more background on Ramalinga Raju and Satyam's history, go to ridingthetiger.com.) Still, we knew what had to be done. We had to grab this tiger by the tail and prevent it from completely devouring everyone and everything in its sight.

Who Is Ramalinga Raju? Reconciling Perception With Reality

Ramalinga Raju was known to the world as being a highly successful leader who was humble, soft-spoken, and of the highest integrity. In 1987, he and a small group of people launched Satyam Computer Services and grew it into a successful global company. Working for Satyam was considered special in Hyderabad—it was, after all, the homegrown success story. Signs throughout the city welcomed Satyam's employees with discounts and favored responses.

In 2005, when we met Raju, he had sold us on the value proposition and the dream of Satyam becoming one of the top companies in the world. And Satyam was already well on its way when we joined it. It had achieved $800 million in revenues and had a staff of more than 20,000. We were so impressed and motivated by what had been accomplished and Raju's incredible vision that we accepted our new roles, sold everything, and moved to India without ever having been there before. We stepped off the airplane in Hyderabad in the middle of the night, and early that same morning, Ed was in the office participating in his first press conference with Raju. More than 40 television stations and newspapers covered the announcement of the Satyam School of Leadership—yet another testament to the admiration all of India felt for Raju.

The Satyam School of Leadership was launched in 2005 and built on the philosophy of expanding the entrepreneurial energy at Satyam to help keep pace with the ever-changing global business context. Ed had been recruited by Raju to design and build the school, including its 240,000-square-foot, state-of-the-art leadership development center. The strategic intent behind its evolution was to create a place to engender leaders who could respond in real time and be consistent in decision making and thus delight stakeholders and be able to work collaboratively in a globally networked environment.

We had also witnessed Raju's generosity in the community. Through three different foundations, he contributed leadership for enhancing education and special programs to assist in modernizing and bringing employment to rural villages. He and his family had funded the Emergency Management and Response Institute, securing 70 state-of-the-art ambulances and 30 acres of land. The institute, which had a uniform toll-free telephone number, "108," across the country, provided emergency services for people caught in life-threatening situations due to accidents or natural calamities. By the end of 2008, the institute had successfully assisted with 350,000 emergencies and in saving about 14,000 lives (Chowdary 2009).

Raju was credited with creating a technology hub in Hyderabad that brought hundreds of thousands of technology jobs to the region. Bill Gates and other corporate dignitaries visited often and marveled at the work being accomplished. Authors wrote about Raju's leadership. Heads of state including former U.S. President Bill Clinton were frequent visitors to the campus. Parents would forbid their children from working elsewhere because they felt it was their duty to give back to Raju for all he had done for Hyderabad. He was an icon for the community.

He demonstrated tremendous support for and pride in learning. He would say, "Satyam is in the business of building leaders." At every new leaders' program, he hosted a dinner where he took several hours to address and engage in dialogue with the participants.

When one was meeting individually with Raju, he would quietly listen, ask a few questions, and then speak about the role science had to play in leadership. He was gracious, supportive, and always complimentary. We had been to his home, spent time with his wife and his sons, and even attended one son's wedding. More than 10,000 people showed up on that extremely hot day to honor Raju's eldest son and his bride. When the temperature sizzled to more than 105 degrees, Raju had personally made sure that misting machines and blowers were strategically placed throughout the covered tents to ensure the comfort of his guests. Everyone perceived him to be both generous and humble.

But now, the unthinkable—certainly, something was wrong; could this all be true? This was a different Raju from the man who had wooed us to join the company and move our family and worldly goods more than halfway around the planet to a country we had never seen. We were numb. What was this deceit from a man everyone had held in such high regard? What about the tens of thousands of people who had been touched by him! What of trust? The irony of the company's name became bittersweet. "Satyam" is a Sanskrit word that means "truth." Was it all a lie? When did it start? Who else was involved? What was to happen to those who gave their loyalty to the company and invested all they had? What would become of us? What would become of Satyam?

We took a deep breath and considered this image: When in the midst of the storm, you see the storm, not the wind, not the rain, not nature bending to the forces. It is only after the storm that you can begin to pick up the pieces. Somehow, something good must come of this catastrophe.

Who Will This Book Benefit?

These days, turbulent times appear to be endemic to the world of business, which is why the principles delineated in this book will be useful for every leader who wants to proactively prepare for the unexpected. Though most books are written from the viewpoint of lessons learned on the path to great success, this book provides a rare opportunity to learn from a catastrophic event that shook the foundation of a thriving global organization. Because this event was so tremendously earth-shattering, we believe the lessons it has taught—the valuable insights and actionable strategies for leaders and change agents as well as professionals involved in learning, human resources, marketing, and business development— can be scaled to assist in creatively making the best of any type of change happening in an organization.

Even though this book primarily reflects our direct experiences during the Satyam Computer Services debacle—wherein the CEO and founder confessed to having "cooked the books" from 2001 to 2008—the time-tested strategies and techniques detailed here are applicable to everyone. The use of Satyam as a case study is relevant because it stretched our leadership abilities to the extreme. That's why we believe this is an important book for business professionals and students alike who want to learn how to reverse a reversal of fortune or to continue on the path of fortune's fortune.

Throughout the book, you are provided with guidelines for leading, templates for planning, and proven ways to apply techniques for leading through learning. The lessons related in this book come from our years of experience working with all kinds of organizations around the world.

Because we have worked with such a variety of clients, the chapters that follow offer guidance that is broadly applicable.

What Will You Learn by Reading This Book?

As a busy professional, you must, of course, budget your time. And this book is well worth your time, because it will give you very useful, pragmatic information on a host of topics concerned with how to lead through learning in turbulent times. You will learn how to maximize tools we have successfully implemented to build social networks, coach leaders, heal the wounded, and salvage customer relationships. For example:

+ We worked with an organization that was about to be acquired by another firm and found that the methods explained in this book eased the transition and prepared both organizational cultures for a successful integration.
+ When we implemented our strategies in a firm that was dealing with turnover rising above 25 percent, the turnover dropped to less than 10 percent within 12 months and remained there for the next five years.
+ We applied these techniques to calm the chaos in organizations after the terrorist attacks on September 11, 2001, in the United States and on July 11, 2006, in India.
+ These practices enhanced the acceptance of change that came about as a result of rapid growth in yet another global firm.

With these cases in mind, let's turn to our first tool: the "Lights On" strategy.

2

The Role of Learning during a Crisis: Developing a "Lights On" Strategy

✦ ✦ ✦

*Angry, panic-stricken, or fearful people may create
the frenzy of activity associated with false urgency,
which can make any situation worse.*

—John Kotter, *A Sense of Urgency*

✦ ✦ ✦

Many organizations underestimate the value and necessity of learning during turbulent times. We learned the hard way that it is not to be forgotten in our experience with Satyam Computer Services. Preparing for a crisis goes far beyond a traditional risk management plan. We would like to say that we were in the minority, that we had proactively developed a learning strategy for leaders to lead through learning—except that we had no plan. Every time the topic had come up, learning was seen as secondary to everything else. Leaders had naïvely indicated that we should stop all training programs until the company recovered. What all of us had failed to realize is that learning can be the very thing that helps stabilize and carry a company through troubled times.

During a corporate crisis, the situation at ground zero is chaotic and not conducive for business as usual. Employee morale is likely to be at an all-time low, the credibility of leadership suffers, employees don't know whom to trust, and feelings of betrayal have left a sour aftertaste. Change happens at lightning speed, information flows in and out of the organization, and the rumor mill cranks up. Learning is critical for stabilizing the organization, providing guidance to leaders, communicating with employees, and keeping the business open.

Immediately following the onset of a corporate crisis, the organization's entire learning group should be convened (virtually and physically). Your goals are to

1. Identify what is known, providing up-to-the-minute details about what has happened, including its impact on the company and its environment, as well as the actions being taken to steady the company.
2. Demonstrate strength and solidarity for the company as you and the learning team build out a new strategy.

For our first meeting after Ramalinga Raju's resignation from the chairmanship of Satyam, we brought together all the leads from the entire learning ecosystem. Because they were scattered throughout the world, the meeting was held virtually, using our webcasting capability. We discussed what was known at the time and began the arduous process of selecting essential services to continue, new services that were necessary, and services that needed to be curtailed. This was the birth of what we came to call our "Lights On" strategy. The situation was surreal. In an instant, the company had gone from hero to zero. We had been plucked from our successful existence and thrust into a crisis. The media were everywhere. They waited outside the gates to the corporate campus, and they called us incessantly. Though we tried to avoid them, they actually did provide many of the details that were lacking at the time. The basic lesson here is that while an organization is on the first 90-day journey through a crisis, its customers need to be retained, its revenues must still be earned, and its projects must continue to be delivered. The learning strategy required is one that helps keep the doors open—the "lights on"—and enables the company to move forward.

The Lights On strategy thus means deciding exactly what must be done to keep the business moving and doing only that which is critical to help the organization to stabilize. Yes, employees need to be comforted, customers need to be retained, and revenues need to be earned. But right now, your priority is to do only what is necessary to keep the organization afloat. Lights On is a process that ensures nothing is forgotten and monitors steps as they are completed efficiently. And with your Lights On template, created in advance, the distribution of the right tasks to the right people is enhanced.

The Lights On plan, which is based on insights from all quarters, has two pillars—learning and communications. The learning pillar includes

+ technology learning
+ domain knowledge
+ people and business leadership
+ completion and closure of existing programs
+ prepaid vendor-supplied programs.

The communications pillar includes

+ regular factual updates
+ differentiating fact from fiction
+ building the confidence of leaders by helping them to communicate and collaborate more effectively.

As a leader, how you react during turbulent times is vital. Your every move will be scrutinized and sooner or later reviewed. But if you follow these steps in developing and implementing the Lights On strategy, you can ensure that nothing is missed:

+ Hold everything.
+ Build a start-stop-continue worksheet.
+ Deploy learning resources optimally.
+ Start an information safari.
+ Include critical communications and bring people together.
+ Develop 30-, 60-, and 90-day scenario plans.

Let's consider each step in detail.

Hold Everything

In times of extreme stress, sometimes you may become so panicked that you forget to breathe. Take a deep breath. Hold it. Exhale. Take one more deep breath, inhaling as much as you can; now hold it; and exhale with a loud sigh. Repeat this every time you need to calm the chaos.

In his book *Winners Never Cheat*, Jon Huntsman (2009, 68) writes, "A crisis allows us the opportunity to dig deep into the reservoirs of our very being, to rise to levels of confidence, strength, and resolve that otherwise we didn't possess. Through adversity we come face to face with who we really are and what really counts."

When faced with turbulence, regardless of the magnitude, the first step is to put everything on hold. Even if only for a few hours, put everything on hold to determine a response. Most likely, the people in the rest of the organization will be doing the same thing as they absorb what has happened. This sounds counterintuitive, but a hasty reaction is not the right response.

Build a Start-Stop-Continue Worksheet

Typically, organizations have a risk plan, yet many do not have a plan beyond protection of stored intellectual capital. A start-stop-continue worksheet assists in approaching the crisis with an intentional map of decisions and options. It is iterative, so you will be revisiting it often, especially while you are on an "information safari," which is covered later in this chapter. The best way to spur your thinking about what to include in this worksheet is to answer these three questions:

+ What must we start doing?
+ What must we stop doing?
+ What must we continue doing?

Notice the use of the word "must." Choosing the "must" tasks prevents people from investing in any superfluous, wasteful activities. Developing this worksheet is thus an essential task that should be undertaken throughout the entire organization. In fact, every leader will find value in writing a "start-stop-continue" worksheet related to their particular area of business.

What Must We Start Doing?

The question, "What must we start doing?" leads to two more questions: "Is the learning absolutely necessary to be able to keep the company open?" and "Is the learning going to help the company get through the turbulence?" If the answer to either of these questions is "yes," and the learning services are not currently in place, then add them to the "start" list. Learning that will help the company stabilize goes right to the top of the list.

What Must We Stop Doing?

The question, "What must we stop doing?" also leads to two more questions: "Is the learning absolutely necessary to be able to keep the company open?" and "Is the learning going to help the company get through the turbulence?" If the answer to these two questions is "no," then stop the service (except in the case of programs in progress for which individual decisions are necessary). Often, a spending freeze may be enacted, allowing only the most critical expenditures to continue being made. Review all scheduled learning to determine its criticality and priority. Nonessential learning should be suspended or canceled.

What Must We Continue Doing?

Finally, the question, "What must we continue doing?" also leads to the same two questions: "Is the learning absolutely necessary to be able to keep the company open?" and "Is the learning going to help the company get through the turbulence?" If the answer to either of these questions is "yes," then these services should be continued. Additionally, consideration needs to be given to learning in progress. In our case, we had certificate and degree programs that would have further affected thousands of employees if they had stopped. Imagine being halfway through an advanced degree program and having it abruptly end. We continued these and allowed participants to select out by choice.

Once you've created a draft, the start-stop-continue worksheet must be reviewed and adjusted, at a minimum, every day.

Deploy Learning Resources Optimally

Armed with the results of your start-stop-continue worksheet exercise, the next step is to create a plan to optimally deploy people and learning resources. Using technology to reach out to people around the world is one efficient method for continuing learning. When optimizing resources, consider the following:

+ Who will develop the learning?
+ What learning will be made available?
+ When will the learning be deployed, and how often?
+ Where will the learning take place—in the classroom, virtually, or by deploying resources to the field?
+ Why is the learning relevant to the current circumstances (see previous start-stop-continue section)?
+ How will the learning be deployed?

With services being started, stopped, and continued, proper realignment of resources is critical. The optimization of your people resources comes from considering the individual strength of the available learning professionals and contributors, diversity of thought and experience, and rapid measures for evaluation of results. In addition, workload balancing needs to be tracked. On a weekly basis, everyone should identify what they have completed and what they are assigned to work on next. Progress should be documented, along with hours worked. This will help to ensure an equitable distribution of work.

Start an Information Safari

Once you have your initial start-stop-continue worksheet and deployment of resources in place, it's time to start your information safari. By collecting information from a multitude of sources, you will gain the depth of knowledge that will enable you to make decisions about direction, services, and actions to meet the changing needs across the organization. There is a tremendous amount of information available during an organization's period of turbulence—ranging from fact to fiction, including financial information, external perceptions, and the reactions of all stakeholders. However, sometimes people get too rushed to take the time to gather information. Other times, people feel they are bothering their stakeholders by asking them for information. Going on an information safari to collect information from a multitude of resources allows for a real response to the corporate crisis. Information, collected on an ongoing basis, is paramount for a successful Lights On plan. During your information safari, you should gather information from learning consultants, points of contact, company leaders and employees, customers, the media, society, and leaders of other companies. Let's briefly consider each of these sources.

Learning Consultants

Embedded within the business units of many organizations are learning consultants. They are responsible for assessment, mapping business objectives to learning needs, and the sourcing of services. These consultants meet regularly with the leaders to whom they are assigned. They learn the business of the business and become trusted advisers and ambassadors. During turbulent times, these consultants need to be seen and heard continuously. They should be on the lookout for changes in the business and regularly (weekly at first) collect start-stop-continue information.

In his book *A Sense of Urgency*, John Kotter (2008, 86) explains: "Insiders learn about the outside and invariably bring some of that back when they return. Information gathered in this way tends, quite naturally, to be given to the other insiders not as antiseptic facts but with stories and with an excitement of distress that affects more than thought. It affects how insiders feel, which (in a head–heart strategy) is so crucial." Asking the start-stop-continue questions discussed previously allows learning and development to respond rather than react. These questions should be asked each time you review the current plan and determine action steps. In addition, leaders and employees should be asked how they are doing, and how they are managing under the current circumstances. Because these questions are asking for a forward view, the learning team can prepare and be there when and as required. For a sense of how one employee asked questions, see the sidebar.

The Voice of Nandini Darsi, Leadership Development Consultant

What could we offer to the leaders, when—clearly—whatever tools we had reinforced earlier did not include managing a crisis of this sort? As I was trying to make sense of my own reactions and fears, the learner in me desired to know what others were thinking. As I spoke with leaders, I found their tone to be "protective" for Satyam. It was heartening to observe that many leaders wanted to step in and help.

Satyam as an organization had invested significantly in learning, and so I asked if learning played a role in their strong demonstration of leadership. Many leaders gave credit to the leadership development we provided, stating that it helped them understand how to "lead from the front, motivate teams, talk, network, and collaborate." We had taught our leaders to think about the impact of their behaviors on others. Some said the learning helped identify inherent strengths. One leader told me, "Leadership training has given me confidence to face any situation, including this one!" It is true that anything you repeat as a mantra gets ingrained in the individual's psyche. . . ."no one wins unless everyone wins" was one such mantra that had penetrated the minds of our leaders.

Here is one example of how we gathered strength from another. My colleague, Nicola Klein, and I launched a training program for a response team on counseling services. The program started right after a critical announcement that was filled with even more bad news. Everyone was shocked. Nicola and I were totally broken inside and forced to face a room full of distraught faces. In my mind, the voice rang again, "What's the point? What can I tell them?" I forced myself to calm down and started the session by saying "I know what you are feeling right now because I feel it too. I am wondering how we can take this session and how we would be able to focus. Let's not park our feelings. Instead, let's identify them, because this is how any individual would be feeling when seeking counseling help."

It's been almost a year since that fateful moment, and most of us are still reflecting on what has happened. Our responsibility as learning professionals is not one to be taken lightly.

Points of Contact

For those business areas where a learning consultant is not assigned or in companies where the learning consultant role does not exist, identify a single point of contact on whom to rely for gathering information from the business and for sending it back to those staff members who are handling the learning and development function. These points of contacts should be individuals who have enough knowledge of the business and relationships to rapidly collect information. The most important factor is constant communication with each.

Company Leaders and Employees

Employees are dealing with their personal, family, and professional concerns. So much is unknown. The "who, what, when, where, and why" questions may not be answered for a long time. In fact, many of them will remain unanswered (see appendix B for the thoughts of some of the affected employees). Regardless of what you know, employees need constant communication and information. Ask employees what they need. Factor in that they often don't know what they need, so you may need to help them. It reinforces that the organization cares and that leaders are there to help them, through good times and bad. Methods you can use to collect information from employees include focus groups, town hall meetings with leaders, surveys, and talking with people one to one and in small groups.

Customers

Customers always have something to say, yet they are seldom asked. They are the best teachers an organization can have. Your customers have the ability to speak about the company where they work, including its culture and leadership, but, more important, they can tell you the experiences they have from working with your company. These lessons are invaluable. Almost immediately after the confession by Ramalinga Raju, learning consultants at Satyam were in touch with leaders assigned to customers to find out what they were saying and doing. We lost many customers, but we retained even more. A few words of encouragement and support from our customers enhanced the motivation of our employees significantly.

Collect their advice and incorporate it into your learning programs. This is covered in more depth in chapter 8.

The Media

If your crisis is large enough to garner media attention, then that is another source to monitor and from which to draw information. During the Satyam crisis, from the minute the news hit the wires, we were in a race with the media to put correct and accurate information out to our employees. That said, the media, with its army of journalists from across India and around the world, uncovered information to which we did not have access. It is imperative to keep up with what the media are saying so that it can be reinforced, clarified, or refuted.

Society

Society is represented by everyone in the communities where you work. At Satyam, we went from being the employer of choice, with our employees receiving preferred treatment and discounts in shops and restaurants, to being looked upon with anger or pity. This plummeting regard will have a great impact on the family and friends of your employees. For that reason, reach out to society to see how leaders can assist, answer questions, and respond to concerns.

Leaders of Other Organizations

There are many leaders—more and more, unfortunately—who have been with a company that got itself into trouble. These people have precious insights to share. Seek out their advice. Integrate their experiences into your plan. A few days after Raju's confession, we posted a message to our LinkedIn network asking leaders around the world to give their advice. We asked them, "What three things should a leader do to help pick up the pieces when his or her organization is faced with deadly turbulence?" Their responses are summarized in chapter 3. When combined with information collected from other sources, the advice from global leaders can help you structure your learning offerings and continuously refine your start-stop-continue worksheet.

Include Critical Communications and Bring People Together

From the onset of the catastrophe, the learning group should be among the most visible across the organization. The group's members may not have all the answers. But they shouldn't duck for cover. One simple and effective way is for the group to run a mailer campaign, sending a daily email that evokes hope, resilience, togetherness, and passion. It should provide guidance, use appropriate humor, and have the goal of motivating a distraught workforce and its equally shattered leadership. These messages are quite powerful. What's important is consistency and immediacy; constant, real-time communication is invaluable.

Employees need to vent, speak without fear, and feel a part of the solution. Leaders need to understand the significance of being "people centered," providing compassion, guidance, and strength. Lao Tzu advises: "To lead people, walk beside them. . . . As for the best leaders, the people do not notice their existence. The next best, the people honor and praise. When the best leader's work is done, the people say, 'We did it ourselves!'" Leaders need to recognize that to lead they must be with their people and must be sensitive to the turmoil and confusion everyone is feeling. For this, at Satyam we launched another email campaign sensitizing leaders and providing simple tools to enhance their listening skills as well as offering guidelines for communicating (such as when to communicate a little, a lot, rather than a lot, a little).

Determining what information is released and to whom is generally determined by a crisis communications team or by the corporate communications department. Information must be communicated, and in some instances it must be protected. Leakage of information to the media in the wrong way can be quite dangerous, as we learned. However, the "orchestrated leakage" of information through the right channels can actually assist.

The learning ecosystem needs to be an integral part of the internal communications plan. Leaders must have the courage to lead from the front, and this is a key area where leading through learning is effective. Often leaders wait to see who will step forward, not realizing all are needed.

When struck by a scandal or crisis, leadership is not determined by rank but by the strength of the talent and conviction to build the relationships necessary to bring about collaboration and seek solutions.

In our situation, leaders came from all areas and from all levels. There was desire, but without knowledge, they required continuous guidance. This is a must-start, high-impact area for learning and development. Learning professionals communicate with leaders, provide advice on how to lead during turbulence, and make available rapid skill enhancement.

Communicate both what is known and what is yet to be known—they are equally important. Information is constantly flowing, and everyone needs to be able to know the difference between fact and fiction; keeping secrets will only lead to rumors.

People need to express themselves; they need the chance to feel a part of the solution. Find ways to bring people together. For example, go out to lunch in small groups, conduct town hall meetings, gather around the water cooler, or lead regular informal web meetings.

During the Satyam crisis, our learning response was a workshop focused on rebuilding the morale of teams. According to Sanjay Devudu, a senior leader with the School of Leadership, who led this morale workshop, "What worked was transparency. Of course, it's never possible to allay everyone's fears; however, being there for our people to provide that support helped. As leaders, we need to address the emotional aspects of people first and then with their help focus on the needs of the business. Every question that was asked was addressed. If we did not have an answer, we were honest enough to admit it. People appreciated that openness and appeared to stay committed to the organization." (For more on these realities, see the following sidebars.)

**Communicating in a Difficult Time:
Lessons Learned by Sanjay Devudu, Senior Leader,
Satyam School of Leadership**

Once the emotional concerns of our own teams were addressed, it was important to keep people engaged in supporting the organization during this difficult time. What actions could we, as learning leaders, take to help tide over the situation? It was also important that we look beyond our own unit/function and consider the bigger picture. Our key lessons included

+ Communicate, communicate, and communicate some more!
+ Deal with emotions first, business issues next.
+ Don't miss the larger picture.
+ Make the necessary tough decisions; let there be no hesitation in doing so.
+ Help other leaders who need the support to tide over the situation.
+ Take care of yourself and one another.
+ Be tuned in to the world around you.

All learning professionals need to take on the additional role of brand ambassador. The internal and external brand will most likely be severely damaged. They need to understand how to interact with the media, how to respond to internal queries, and, most important of all, how to remain calm in the face of uncertainty. During our first meeting after the news broke, a learning professional asked, "If we are to take care of everyone else, who will take care of us?" We responded, "We must take care of each other." This is accomplished through daily updates, regular meetings, informal gatherings at the coffee station, and frequent impromptu celebrations of even the smallest successes.

The function of the morale workshop was to provide the opportunity for employees to voice their fears and explore new paths together. Employees were asked to step into three roles during the workshop: employees, consultants, and think like the CEO.

For the first role—employees—participants voiced their fears by writing them on Post-it notes (virtually or in person) and then placing them on charts located around the room. Small teams organized them into themes and reported out to the larger group. These formed the basis for many of the frequently asked questions that were concurrently developed for the company intranet.

For the second role—consultants—participants removed their employee hat and donned the hat of consultant. We asked them, "As consultants to this organization, how would you go about rebuilding?" Then we used the same format as described for the first role. Post-it notes were written and placed around the room and then organized and reviewed in small teams. This information can be disseminated to all leaders across the organization.

For the third role—think like the CEO—participants donned the hat of CEO. We asked them, "As CEO for this organization, how would you go about triaging, treating, and rebuilding?" This advice, when consolidated, could have been presented to the CEO or the crisis leadership team. In our case, the information was presented to our new CEO.

Open and Transparent Communication

For the first two weeks of the Satyam crisis, we had multiple updates throughout the day and a daily call. Even when there wasn't much to report, people still had questions. It was clear that they looked forward to having regular access to their leaders and to each other. They felt comfort in being with each other. Because the team was scattered around the world, we brought them together both physically and virtually. We kept them informed, and all our leaders opened their doors. They each proactively met with members of their teams. Each day the leaders came together, and we discussed how everyone was doing and our next steps.

We quickly realized how essential learning was going to be to help salvage the company. We provided the necessary light to guide others—we became the communication vehicle for leaders to work with their teams to survive. Partnering with the corporate communications team and human resources team, we pooled resources and discussed steps toward recovery. We were the first to come forward, and we led the charge for many weeks, providing information, coaching, and support across the global organization.

We spoke candidly about our fears and pledged to share information as it became available. We also agreed to regular updates even if there was nothing to share. We realized how important it was to reach beyond our group, to engage other leaders who would need support to speak with their teams.

Our families had to be told. As a culture, Indians feel shame when associated with such matters, even to the point of seeing this as a personal failure. The loss would be tremendous, almost unbearable to some. We had much to do. We went live with these same candid conversations the day following Raju's announcement on our web television station (see chapter 6). Every associate around the world would hear our fears and our stories about how we communicated with our friends and families (especially those of us with children). These programs were available to all 53,000 employees, reaching out to everyone in many different ways. Where before a crisis may have closed our doors, we recognized the need to use our learning methods, both formal and informal, to reach anyone with access to a computer. We became the Satyam Emergency Broadcast Network. We were applauded for our honesty and courage. It was a great and fulfilling experience to be able to mobilize the talents and capabilities of a group of incredibly dedicated professionals to leverage learning and development during this challenging time.

Develop 30-, 60-, and 90-Day Scenario Plans

You will recall that we said the Lights On plan is iterative and additive. Once the initial crisis has occurred, triaging, treating, and rebuilding require the addition of 30-, 60-, and 90-day plans. The process of building these plans should start with answering these questions:

+ What is known?
+ What is probable?
+ What is unknown?

First, respond to each question from the perspective of the organization. Another information safari is called for here. Second, develop the learning and development 30-, 60-, and 90-day scenario plans.

In developing these plans, first observe the immediate "shock wave," and then create a scenario plan for all possible paths—such as

+ The company might continue and rebuild on its own.
+ The company might close.
+ The company might be taken over by the government.
+ The company might be sold.
+ The new owner's processes and policies might be implemented.

+ There might be a transition among employees—in the case of the company being taken over, employees would literally be given new identities.
+ New branding might be needed.
+ There might potentially be an entirely new board of directors.
+ There might be a new management team.
+ There might be a reshuffling of roles.
+ There might be customer attrition.
+ There might be employee transitions.
+ There could be a desire for employee retention.
+ There will be employee uncertainty and a need for extensive communication.
+ There will be the potential for a large-scale layoff.
+ There will be survivor programs for those who retain their positions.
+ There will be a need to rebuild teams.
+ There will be a need to protect intellectual capital.
+ There will be a need to rebuild trust.

If your crisis or challenging situation is large enough to garner media attention, keep an eye on what is being reported. This information is useful for scenario planning. The media proved to be an excellent source of ongoing information for us. Throughout, the media, with their reporting of the facts and conjectures, appeared to have access to information much faster than we did.

Leaders need advice to properly care for the wounded (see chapter 7). This includes advice from other leaders, employees, families, investors, customers, and the community. In situations like this, the staff may need to be prepared for the follow-up investigation—people requesting documents and information. There are many more areas that need to be on the "start" list, each unique to the circumstances. Now let's look more closely at how to best develop 30-, 60-, and 90-day scenario plans.

The 30-Day Plan

The 30-day scenario plan is detailed in table 2-1. Some of your 30-day priorities may include

Table 2-1. The 30-Day Scenario Plan

Organization's Answer to Questions, and Learning Response	Questions to Ask in Plan-Building Process		
	What Is Known?	What Is Probable?	What Is Unknown?
Organization's answer	Employees are frightened	Organization will most likely continue	Change in ownership
Learning response	Three-roles workshop	Ongoing communication	Not likely during first 30 days
Organization's answer	Loss of customers	Redeployment of employees	Actions of government
Learning response	Customer retention communication in partnership with marketing and communications departments, broadcast on web TV	Reskilling programs for impacted employees	Revisit daily; be ready for communication

+ Hear the voices of all stakeholders.
+ Bring calm to the chaos.
+ Build the communication skills of leaders (internal and external).
+ Manage the crisis—financial, physical, behavioral. This includes processes for securing funding, the parameters within which learning can and cannot take place, and the key timely messages to be repeatedly communicated.
+ Evaluate current knowledge versus knowledge needed, followed by a collective and individual assessment of skill strengths and gaps.
+ Start career counseling, résumé writing, and outplacement services for those displaced.
+ Provide coaching for everyone (see chapter 5).
+ Start a "help line" with resources available inside and outside the organization to handle stress-related symptoms.
+ Switch to virtual learning delivery as much as possible to ensure that all employees have access.
+ Rebuild the brand internally and externally.
+ Document and archive intellectual property.
+ Enhance the usage of learning technologies, with an emphasis on communications (see chapter 6).
+ Know what success looks like.

The 60-Day Plan

Leadership decisions, potential ownership decisions, customer retention, and additional impact begin to reveal themselves in about 60 days. Preparing for new leadership and/or ownership (especially when senior leaders are the cause) entails

+ taking an inventory of service offerings
+ preparing for a collaborative effort in case of new ownership, where cultures will be merged
+ possibly transitioning employees to a new company, which would include learning a new "history"

✦ communicating with all existing employees.

During any type of crisis caused by or involving leaders, trust will be affected. The needs to assess and rebuild trust are discussed in detail in chapters 3 and 4. A strong "let's get to know one another" and "let's rebuild together" focus needs to be put in place. A behavioral approach to the work/life balance should be addressed in the 60-day plan.

The 90-Day Plan

After about 90 days, with new ownership or new leadership potentially in place, customer, employee, and investor retention continues as the organization rebuilds its brand. Learning priorities at this time become

✦ Communicate new or changed human resources practices.
✦ Continue to assist displaced employees.
✦ Rebuild teams in a smaller, more consolidated environment.
✦ Revise the induction program to match the new leadership or ownership.
✦ Rebuild the brand or begin to rebrand.
✦ Facilitate strategies that ensure the long-term retention of people.
✦ Implement solid people-centered strategies. For instance, provide opportunities for employees to voice their fears and concerns by setting up a feedback email address or using anonymous surveys and soliciting information during informal conversations.

Once you have developed solid 30-, 60-, and 90-day scenario plans, you are ready for a real-time response and the return to long-term strategic planning (see chapters 8 and 9).

Key Points

The key points for the role of learning during a crisis:

✦ Many, if not most organizations, underestimate the value and necessity of learning during a crisis.
✦ During a corporate crisis, the situation at ground zero is chaotic and not conducive for business as usual.

- Immediately following the onset of a corporate crisis, identify what is known and ask learning professionals to demonstrate strength and solidarity for the company as you develop a new learning strategy.
- The learning strategy required is one that helps keep the doors open, the lights on, and the company moving forward.
- Following the Lights On strategy means deciding exactly what must be done to keep the business moving and doing only that which is critical to help the organization to stabilize.
- When faced with turbulence, regardless of the magnitude, the first step is to put everything on hold.
- Develop a "response worksheet" that answers three questions: What must we start doing? What must we stop doing? What must we continue doing?
- Communicate what is known and what is yet to be known—both are equally important.
- Optimization of people resources comes from considering the individual strength of the learning professionals and contributors, diversity of thought and experience, and rapid measures for evaluation of results.
- Going on an information safari to collect information from a multitude of resources allows for a real response to a corporate crisis. This safari should include learning consultants, points of contact, leaders (internal and external), employees, customers, media, and society.
- From day one of the catastrophe, the learning group should be the among the most visible across the organization.
- In addition to speaking with employees, leaders require assistance to articulate ways of explaining what is happening to their families and friends.
- Leaders need to understand the significance of being "people centered," providing compassion, guidance, and strength.
- Once the initial crisis has occurred, triaging, treating, and rebuilding requires the development of 30-, 60-, and 90-day scenario plans, which starts with finding answers to three questions: What is known? What is probable? What is unknown?

3

The Role of Leadership in Turbulent Times: Setting Guidelines for Key Concerns

✦ ✦ ✦

Don't let the news of today undo the successes of yesterday or tomorrow.

—Howard Richmond, MD

✦ ✦ ✦

During turbulent times, everything speeds up. The pressures of shifting emotions, processes, and demands increase as more and more is expected from everyone. You are simultaneously juggling the daily needs of the business, caring for the wounded, and helping pick up the pieces. Because these difficult periods are stressful, leaders must rapidly and proactively convert emotions into actions. Leaders must concurrently take care of themselves and everyone else. This takes time, patience, empathy, a willingness to shift priorities, and communication—constant communication, even "overcommunication." The leaders who lead "out loud"—those who maintain transparency, approachability, and integrity—are the ones with whom people want to work, in good times and bad. And these are the leaders whom others seek to become.

After our CEO at Satyam, Ramalinga Raju, confessed his malfeasance, the entire situation was surreal. We went from a celebrated company to being immersed in scandal. The huge scale and impact of Satyam's downfall were clear in the headline of *The Economist*'s cover story: "India's Enron," and *BusinessWeek* featured a photo of Raju on the cover with the headline "From Icon to I Con." So began the journey toward a different strategy for leaders, which included new behaviors, competencies, and expectations to control the damage and rebuild what could be rebuilt. Leaders went on autopilot when it came to management; they went to work assessing the situation, implementing customer-retention measures, and shoring up the business. However, these same leaders were unsure how to handle the people and relationship issues. This was not due to a lack of desire. It was more about the lack of comfort that comes from having to communicate, empathize, and support people throughout a difficult time. And this was a time when our employees most needed those things. Neglecting your employees during a crisis is a mistake and can lead to a backlash—so ensure that your leaders are equipped to care for their people.

12 Leadership Guidelines

The approach that works best in this situation is leading through learning—which primarily entails developing leadership guidelines. It is simple and powerful. Leverage learning to assist leaders with the complicated people and relationship dimensions of the business. Develop a set of leadership guidelines. Communicate and teach them to all leaders. Use these guidelines as the basis for coaching conversations. We developed 12 guidelines as part of our leading through learning strategy. Use these guidelines as a basis for your strategy, or adapt them to your unique situation:

1. Understand that we will *never* get back to normal.
2. Take care of one another.
3. React . . . pause . . . respond.
4. Talk—even when you don't believe there is much to say.
5. Be visible—now is not the time to play hide-and-seek.
6. Maintain integrity and high moral values.

7. Optimize costs, with retention in mind.
8. Be a brand ambassador.
9. Assess and rebuild trust.
10. Remember, leaders are human, too.
11. Think like a child.
12. Take care of your emotional, physical, and spiritual well-being.

Let's look at each of these guidelines.

Understand That We Will *Never* Get Back to Normal

Organizations are constantly in the process of evolving to something new. An organization in crisis creates revolutionary change, resulting in radical shifts occurring much faster than most people are comfortable handling. It's natural to want a return to the status quo. But no matter how devastating the situation, there is opportunity in a crisis. At the heart of a crisis is learning. There were things that were once considered "normal" that helped pitch your organization into turbulence. This is your opportunity to see those things for the mistakes they were and begin to build better practices.

The only constant about "normal" is that it is always changing. So instead of hoping for and trying to get back to normal, you need to move on, seek better ways to do things, and let these new ways become the new normal.

Take Care of One Another

Leaders must demonstrate emotional intelligence—transparency, empathy, patience, forgiveness, and inclusivity. They are obliged to look for ways to take care of one another. As a leader, first and foremost, explore your own feelings. Find someone with whom you can speak, someone who has an objective view and who provides you with empathic listening. At work, don't be reticent to express your feelings, and allow others to express their feelings without judgment. Words like "hurt," "worried," "cheated," "shock," and "disbelief" will be spoken, along with phrases like "How did this happen?" and "Am I going to lose my job?" Let them flow. There is no need to always have an answer or even a reply. This is the time to be a great listener and to exhibit empathy. Use paraphrasing to let others know you have heard them. People need to verbalize their thoughts and feelings to work through them. They want to be heard and need to feel heard. The simple act of listening rapidly reduces anxiety.

This is the time to bring everyone together; have them talk about where they were when the news first came out (if an event caused the crisis). Provide regular updates on what's happening across the organization. Expand inclusivity. Inclusive management allows the diversity of talents within an organization to be recognized, utilized, and rewarded. Here are some basic guidelines for immediately bringing about more inclusivity:

+ *Rotate management.* You have the opportunity to observe leadership and empower it. Consider rotating management routinely, perhaps on a monthly basis, giving individuals the time to "try on" the new role and to be successful.

+ *Solicit input without prejudice.* This is challenging and has significant rewards. If your team is empowered to openly share innovative approaches, knowing that their ideas are seen as having value significantly motivates people.

+ *Enable the minority voice to be heard.* Ensure that everyone's voice is given time and real attention, recognizing that the group's consensus is not always the right answer. Provide a sounding board for new ideas that are not reached through a "consensus rules" approach. The imperative here is to ensure that the minority voice is not lost.

+ *Provide an opportunity for someone in the group to give a summary of ideas.* Take the necessary time to discuss what worked in the meeting and what did not, acknowledging those who contributed and the collaborative efforts of the group. Don't forget to identify what can be done to improve the process in the future.

+ *Meet informally.* A five-minute coffee break, potluck lunch, mini-retreat, or offsite seminar gives people an opportunity to align with the organization's vision and objectives and celebrate their successes. Honor contributions publicly, and make certain that the acknowledgment is documented for yearly appraisals.

✦ *Get rid of or build connecting tunnels in silos.* For instance, when one department begins to focus only on its specific needs and becomes territorial, provide the opportunity to collaborate on projects. Organize a monthly memo or newsletter. Call attention to collaboration between groups and showcase the bigger picture—the tie-in to organizational goals.

✦ *Get rid of the skunks.* If you go into a room with a skunk, everyone comes out smelling like one. This phrase was often repeated by Susan Cipollini, our longtime friend and colleague. If someone isn't contributing or they are sabotaging outcomes (passively or aggressively), get rid of them. Keeping this individual in the group can destroy morale, and it sends an inappropriate message that your leadership is complacent.

React . . . Pause . . . Respond

For safety and expediency, leaders are counted on to react. Adrenaline pushes energies to parts of the body most required to handle the turbulence. Your mind might be more alert, thinking at a rapid speed, eyes dilated so you can see better, and hearing sharpened—and all this may bring on the "normal" reaction: fight or flight. When you react in that moment, a normal response, it may or may not be right. Pause. Reflect. Then collect as much information as possible, and consider the benefits and consequences of each possible course of action before deciding on the next thing to do.

The enterprise's response is critical for leaders to consider. As a leader, you face your own turmoil while the collective enterprise also faces its own. Thus the leader must balance his or her concerns with those of the organization by recognizing this duality and separating personal responses from business responses. For example, as a leader, you must take decisive action to help the company recover and care for others (see chapter 7). Yet as an individual, you must decide how you will respond by taking into consideration all the factors at that time, including your career desires, personal needs, and family situation. No matter how you respond, it will be right for you as long as it comes from information gathering, integrity, an open heart, and seeking to understand.

Talk—Even When You Don't Believe There Is Much to Say

I don't know what to say.
Everyone is getting information daily from the company.
They can see it on the news.

The statements above are just some of the excuses leaders provide when asked why they are not communicating with their teams. There is no such thing as overcommunicating, especially during times of rapid change. No one has a valid excuse for not communicating. Provide regular updates as often as necessary. When Raju's confession set off a crisis of massive proportions, updates were held every hour. Then we shifted to updates every few hours and then to updates daily and weekly.

Never cancel an update. This scares people. Even when there isn't much to report, people appreciate being told what is known again and again. They also appreciate the opportunity to ask you questions. They feel more connected to you and the organization with regular access.

What may in normal times be seen as overcommunication is good communication during turbulent times. You are communicating enough when people repeat your words to each other and to you. Consistent and continuous messaging prevents the rumor mill from gearing up and demonstrates leaders' approachability, transparency, and heartfelt concern.

Be Visible—Now Is Not the Time to Play Hide-and-Seek

I have my own stress to deal with.
I have incredibly tight deadlines.
I have no time to hangout and talk to people.

The statements above are just a few of the excuses you will hear. It's true that leaders are tremendously busy working to stabilize the company, have additional requirements placed on their shoulders, and are anxious themselves, but the need of the hour is still the team's. When the leader goes into hiding, people become fearful. They question what is happening, and without the leader's presence, they might even make up the story for him or her. This is how dangerous rumors and urban legends are born.

Now is not the time to hide away at home or in your office. Closed doors make people nervous. Open the door, get up from your desk, walk around, and talk with people; let them know you care. During the Satyam scandal, a colleague sent this quotation (we tried to find out who wrote it and couldn't): "They don't care how much you know until they know how much you care." Listen, empathize, share advice, provide words of comfort; just be there. You may be injured; we all are. You may have a lot of work to get done; we all do. Be present, inform, comfort, and provide strength for others.

Maintain Integrity and High Moral Values

During turbulent times, leaders will have to take measures that they might not feel good about. There may be a pending layoff or a potential sale of the company, or quite possibly something even worse set to happen. Current circumstances should not influence, broaden, or distort your definition of integrity and other core values.

Optimize Costs, with Retention in Mind

The most common mistake leaders make during any kind of turbulence is implementing cost optimization, which often includes layoffs, without considering the retention of staff. Cost optimization should be discussed and implemented concurrently with a retention plan. If you must optimize costs, then simultaneously work to retain your best people. Your organization will emerge stronger. During and after turbulent times, retention should be one of the highest priorities. You should make cost optimization decisions, keeping in mind their impact on retention. This information allows you to assess risk and make more informed decisions.

Be a Brand Ambassador

The temptation during crisis is to tell everyone everything—the good, the bad, the ugly. Though transparency and adherence to core values is necessary, especially when leading through turbulence, the organization and its people need leaders who are brand ambassadors. As brand ambassadors, you are responsible for representing the organization both internally and externally in a positive manner. This does not mean stretching the truth. It simply means that you should refrain from making negative statements that might cause further turbulence. It also means seeking advice from your marketing and communications group on when and how to inter-face with the media and providing consistent messages to everyone.

Assess and Rebuild Trust

Mahatma Gandhi wrote, "In the attitude of silence the soul finds the path in a clearer light, and what is elusive and deceptive resolves itself into crystal clearness. Our life is a long and arduous quest after truth." There are many advantages to being a part of an environment that is built on truth. People are more open, and there is greater productivity, less internal competitiveness, stronger relationships, and overall a more positive atmosphere. All stakeholders—from employees to customers, investors, and society—know when they are working with an organization built on trust. That said, damage control and rebuilding a seriously injured organization require difficult decisions that not everyone will understand. For this reason, you and the other leaders in your organization must continuously assess and rebuild trust. Seneca, the Roman philosopher and writer (4 BCE–65 CE), taught that "no one can be happy who has been thrust outside the pale of truth. And there are two ways that one can be removed from this realm: by lying, or by being lied to."

Can trust be rebuilt? It depends. People trust the trusted. In her article "Trust Fall," Pat Galagan (2009, 26–28) notes that "there are some who believe that organizations must do more than apologize and be truthful about past sins. The leadership experts James O'Toole and Warren Bennis caution that trust requires more than honest behavior from leaders. Rather, it takes cultures that reward honesty and punish dishonesty." Galagan continues with a quotation from O'Toole and Bennis: "A new metric of corporate leadership will be the extent to which executives create organizations that are economically, ethically, and socially sustainable." We will discuss this further in chapter 4.

Remember, Leaders Are Human, Too

Crisis and turbulence bring out both the best and worst in each of us. When your organization is facing difficult times, you go through a lot. You may feel hurt, damaged, worried—and that's just the tip of the emotional iceberg. Sometimes you won't be at your best, although it is important for you, as the leader, to hold it together as much as possible. A story illustrates this reality.

Ed experienced the need to be strong for everyone during his final trip to India as chief learning officer for Satyam. We had lived in India for almost four years and faced many challenges and celebrated many accomplishments. We had been immersed in the culture and become a part of many families from India and around the world.

On October 23, 2009, Ed attended his final meeting with what is now known as the Mahindra Satyam Learning World—the Mahindra Group having bought Satyam in April 2009. He thanked everyone for allowing him to be the leader of such an amazing team. He told them this:

> While it is true most of us have moved out [the team had reduced from close to 400 to 75 people], you should not feel sad. We came together to help grow a magnificent global company. We achieved the top honor in learning, the ASTD BEST Award—the only company outside the United States to ever achieve number 1. During the crisis, we came together. . . . We implemented the Lights On strategy, expanded our communications with web television and radio, and carried messages of hope to the people. . . . We contributed our expertise to begin the journey to restore employee and customer confidence, which we knew would ultimately restore our investors' confidence and regain the support of society. . . . Most of us have or are moving on to other organizations. I know this feels poignant; however, consider this: . . . We are a field of perennial flowers. This is our autumn, [when] flowers dry and turn to seed. The seeds catch the wind, spreading far and wide. They lay dormant for the winter. Spring comes, the weather changes, everything awakens, seeds pushing through the earth, . . . [and] they blossom into beautiful flowers. . . . As we venture from this place, we are those seeds spreading far and wide. When you land, take time to acclimate to your new environment. Then grow, blossom, and convey lessons to the world. . . . This is not our ending. This is our beginning.

Most people there thought Ed put on a very brave face. As he had always done, he offered himself authentically to the team. At that moment, he felt reconciled, settled, and content. Nevertheless, posttraumatic stress eventually sets in for everyone. While in India, he fooled himself into believing his wounds had healed. But back in the United States, separated from everyone and unemployed, his journey of pain continued—he was beset by a lack of energy, loss of confidence, and overwhelming sadness. It was time for him to heed the Chinese proverb, "To get through the hardest journey, we need take only one step at a time, but we must keep on stepping." It was his turn to take one step. Remember, leaders are human, too.

Think Like a Child

The guideline to think like a child may seem out of place—how could that help, particularly during turbulent times? But when you think about it, children do not carry the same burdens as adults; they live in the moment and, especially when very young, are constantly playing (figure 3-1). They

Figure 3-1. *Four Boys from the Local Orphanage, with Priscilla, on Their First-Ever Trip to the Airport.* (Photograph courtesy of Ed Cohen.)

may sense your sadness or turmoil. They may even ask you about it. Children allow you to take the opportunity to see the big picture; they provide a goal for you to get through things. They simplify everything, and this allows you to stop overanalyzing and complicating matters. Soon they will be running around, playing their games. Join them, the time will pass, and you will have a much-needed break.

Try it. Live "in the moment" as children tend to do, and surrender to your playful inner child for a short period. This will remind you of the significance of taking time to tune out and not allow business to consume every moment. Work/life balance can still exist, even in a crisis.

Take Care of Your Emotional, Physical, and Spiritual Well-Being

Your health—your emotional, physical, and spiritual well-being—is important all the time, and it is critical during turbulent times. Don't put any aspect of your well-being on hold. You will feel like ignoring your needs—but don't! Calm your mind at night. Get a good night's sleep. If you need to talk with someone, seek a counselor, a coach, or your best friend. Start or continue an exercise routine. Be more mindful of your diet. And look for the comfort that comes from following your own spiritual path. This is not an easy task for most leaders, who become so consumed by their professional responsibilities that they sacrifice everything else. Change and uncertainty at work are draining, but you cannot allow them to take over your life.

Summing Up: Listening to the Voices of Global Leaders

At this point, it's useful to bring in our findings from our survey of global leaders to recapitulate the importance of developing guidelines like the ones we've described above. We asked the members of our global network to provide their advice on what leaders should do during turbulent times. We received 193 responses in less than one week using LinkedIn—social networking definitely helped us. Leaders from 19 countries around the world responded, with varying numbers of years experience: 4 percent had less than five years, 15 percent had 5 to 10 years, 50 percent had 11 to 20 years, 22 percent had 21 to 30 years, and 9 percent had more than 30 years. These leaders were in industries ranging from banking and finance to consulting, real estate, retail, and public services. More than half were senior managers, and a third were senior executives. As one leader—Octavio Ballesta, a corporate strategist and management consultant from Venezuela—expressed it succinctly, "[in] the current economic downturn, [there] are five critical areas for leaders when managing a crisis":

✦ *Boldness:* Leaders should have the courage to recognize their mistakes, misconceptions, and poor decisions.

✦ *Proactivity:* Leaders need to use their skills, knowledge, influence, and experience to anticipate problems and devise contingency plans.

✦ *Effective and pragmatic communication:* Leaders must find the right spokespeople to effectively convey key information to the media.

✦ *Leverage experts:* Leaders may need to hire expert public relations and change management consultants to help guide the organization.

✦ *Purpose and focus:* Leaders should lead through their influence—with functional knowledge, a strategic mindset, and a willingness to coach employees.

In addition, we received advice on these topics from the global leaders:

✦ *Be visible and communicate often*—this isn't the time to hunker down. Be available to your staff—prepare to answer questions, sell the strategy, and let them know what's working.

✦ *Tell it like it is*—be honest, even about the scary bad stuff.

✦ *Have a plan*, and have the confidence to revise the plan as the situation unfolds.

✦ *Get your leaders out*—to communicate the plan face to face, in straightforward words. People feel more confident with a map—even if it may need to change.

✦ *Make sure your internal and external communications teams talk with each other and coordinate their information,* so your staff does not receive any mixed or contradictory messages.

✦ *There are only so many strategies for handling corporate crises;* it's how thoughtfully you implement them that makes the difference.

In their responses, the global leaders used a number of terms and phrases, which are useful to briefly mention, in summary:

✦ *Communication*—includes integrity, honestly, transparency, and setting expectations.

✦ *Revisit your core purpose*—includes your core values, vision, and retrospect.

✦ *Focus on employee confidence*—includes employee morale, staff and customer retention, and motivation.

✦ *Engage key stakeholders*—includes investor and media relations, collaboration, and listening to ideas.

✦ *Sanitize the organization*—includes conducting an internal investigation, identifying of root causes, and preventing future incidents.

✦ *Protect market share and customer retention*—includes evaluating losses and your market retention strategy.

✦ *Leadership behavior*—includes remaining calm, being visible and accessible, leading by example, and demonstrating optimism, courage, and boldness.

✦ *Strategic foresight*—includes short- and long-term financial, people, and business planning.

✦ *Rebuild the brand*—includes rebuilding trust and confidence, internally and externally, to demonstrate renewed commitment and passion.

✦ *Accept responsibility*—includes the willingness to be accountable as a leader and as an organization (no matter who is responsible for causing the turbulence).

Key Points

Key points for the role of leadership during a crisis:

+ During turbulent times, leaders must rapidly and proactively convert emotions into actions.
+ Turbulent times are stressful. Leaders must concurrently take care of themselves and everyone else.
+ Understand that we will *never* get back to normal.
+ Find ways to take care of each other.
+ React . . . pause . . . respond.
+ Talk, even when you don't believe there is much to say.
+ Be visible—now is not the time to play hide-and-seek.
+ Maintain integrity and high moral values.
+ Optimize costs, with retention in mind.
+ Be a brand ambassador.
+ Assess and rebuild trust.
+ Remember, leaders are human, too.
+ Think like a child.
+ Take care of your emotional, physical, and spiritual well-being.
+ Collaborate to build and communicate a solid plan for the future.
+ Communicate in straightforward words to all stakeholders.
+ People feel more confident knowing there is a plan.

4

Guiding the Evolution of Your Organization's Culture

✦ ✦ ✦

Organizational cultures are created by leaders, and one of the most decisive functions of leadership may well be the creation, the management, and—if and when that may become necessary—the destruction of culture.

—Edgar Schein

✦ ✦ ✦

Throughout an organization's life, additional norms, behaviors, and practices creep in. This reality is even more pronounced during turbulent times. Positive behaviors may include greater pride, fierce loyalty to the organization, a stronger work ethic, broader collaboration, and boosted collegiality. Negative behaviors may include fear, distrust, and anger that results in hoarding of information and unhealthy internal competition. Together, both positive and negative behaviors change the organizational culture.

Charles Hill and Gareth Jones (2001, 396) define organizational culture as the "beliefs and ideas about what kinds of goals members of an organization should pursue and ideas about the appropriate kinds or standards of behavior organizational members should use to achieve these goals. From organizational values develop organizational norms, guidelines, or expectations that prescribe appropriate kinds of behavior by employees in particular situations and control the behavior of organizational members towards one another." Unfortunately, countless leaders do not recognize the influence that organizational culture has on the past, present, and future accomplishments of their enterprise. Even more important is their lack of understanding about how they influence the culture.

Culture: Conscious or Accidental?

Every organization develops both a conscious and an accidental culture. Its conscious culture unfolds from the written and spoken goals, values, behaviors, and practices that are taught, measured, and reinforced in the organization. However, think about where you work: Are particular behaviors and norms that are not in writing passed on from one generation to the next, from one employee to the next? This is called the accidental culture. It emerges from the unwritten and unspoken values, behaviors, and practices to which everyone knows they should adhere. When asked about this culture, no one can articulate where it is written; they just recognize it, as if by symbiosis. This accidental culture is revealed with seeming randomness over the course of the organization's history. Collectively, a conscious culture and an accidental culture permeate every nook of every organization. And in both forms, the organizational culture has the power to positively and negatively influence the actions of leaders and the performance of employees, along with the retention and attraction of employees and customers. A conscious culture has many benefits:

+ Leaders more rapidly assimilate to the culture.
+ Employees more quickly understand the range of acceptable behaviors.
+ Recruitment is made easier.

+ When there is a lack of fit, it is easier to identify and take action.
+ The likelihood of successful integration in the case of a merger or acquisition increases.
+ And most important, systemic change is easier because there is no battle between the conscious and accidental cultures.

Satyam: A Case Study of Cultural Development

From its inception in 1987, Satyam Computer Systems' core purpose was known as "AICS Delight"—with "AICS" standing for associates (who include both employees and suppliers), investors, customers, and society. The premise: Put associates first, and they would delight the rest of the stakeholders. Though many processes and procedures (such as slow reimbursement of expenses and last-minute decisions) contradicted this, Satyam was, for all intents and purposes, a people-centered culture. A cultural mismatch stemmed from the fact that Satyam was entrenched in a hierarchical, largely patriarchal organizational culture, in which all major decisions were primarily made by the chairman and other decisions were made by the top leaders.

Then, in 2005, there was a sea change. With the launch of its School of Leadership, Satyam began to shift away from patriarchal leadership to a more distributed leadership model, which was called Full Life-Cycle Leadership. The business was divided into logical parts called full life-cycle businesses. Leaders were empowered to run these businesses, and they in turn passed down decisions and empowerment to their employees. People appreciated and were motivated by this new form of leadership. Turnover, which had exceeded 20 percent, dropped to about 10 percent and remained that low for the next four years. What's ironic is that Full Life-Cycle Leadership was conceived and developed by Ramalinga Raju, Satyam's chairman, even while he continued to "cook the books." When the world learned of his accounting fraud, the company reverted to patriarchal leadership. This was a very interesting turn of events. Employees were lost without the direction of their patriarchal top leader, and only a few other leaders had the courage to step forward. The cognitive dissonance resulting from the disclosure of the fraud was more than many could grasp. The firm's leaders were paralyzed, and very few decisions were being made.

45

The culture of the geographical region significantly affects an organization's culture. Thus, as an organization headquartered in South India, Satyam was influenced and shaped by the dichotomy resulting from the confluence of a very traditional, largely Hindu culture and an increasingly modern culture. We spent four years living in Hyderabad. We attended many marriages, participated in local festivals, and formed wonderful friendships that we are certain will last a lifetime (figure 4-1). Although we realize that four years was not long enough to call ourselves experts, during our time there, we sought to keenly observe the people and the influences of India's culture. India is not only the world's second most populous modern nation, with 1.2 billion people, but it is also one of the world's oldest continuous civilizations, with more than 5,000 years of history. Though most of the country practices Hinduism, there are also many other religions—including Islam, Buddhism, and Christianity. Religion is highly integrated into the fiber of the people, and it keenly influences organizational culture.

We actually moved to India—selling our home, vehicles, and most of our possessions—without ever having been there (figure 4-2). When we contemplated our move, we were apprehensive about our inability to speak Hindi. We were told not to worry, because India is also the largest English-speaking country in the world. However, though this fact is correct, it is somewhat misleading. We had failed to do the math. This statistical result is achieved because India has three times as many people as

Figure 4-1. *Attending the Marriage of Sunita and Natraj.* (Photograph courtesy of Ed Cohen.)

Figure 4-2. *MacKenzie Cohen, Apprehensive about Moving to India, Waits at the Airport.* (Photograph courtesy of Ed Cohen.)

the United States, though only one-third of its population speaks English. When we moved to India, we discovered the reality that less than half the people we encountered spoke any English. We also learned that more than 30 languages are spoken across its various regions. For example, in Hyderabad, the primary language is Telugu. It was interesting to see how the diversity of languages influenced Satyam's organizational culture in its many offices. As we traveled from office to office around the Indian subcontinent, Hindi was the primary language spoken, but local languages were used as much.

The diversity of languages in India's regions reflects the nation's overall historical development—the regions were part of British India or separate princely states until the nation's independence and unification starting in 1947. Thus, each region has its own history, its own festivals, and its own culture. East, west, north, and south, the people are different, and their traditions—though broadly similar, given such common factors as Hinduism—are nonetheless diverse. That said, tightly knit extended families remain commonplace around the country. Grandparents, parents, aunts, uncles, brothers, sisters, and cousins all live together. Parents shape and in some cases make most decisions for their children, ranging from what and where to study to whom to work for and whom to marry. In fact, several times, when a team member was doing exceptionally well, we were encouraged to call his or her parents to let them know. After one of those calls, an employee showed up at the office the next day with his entire family. That's right—his mother, father, grandparents, some aunts, uncles, brothers, sisters, and cousins all presented themselves to show their appreciation because we had shown ours. There are few places in the world where this kind of highly traditional familial behavior is witnessed today, and it, of course, shapes organizations' cultures.

In India, leaders, especially CEOs, are held in the highest regard—something like a supreme patriarch. They are treated as deities, and many people blindly follow them. So, when Ramalinga Raju walked into a room, everyone stood to demonstrate reverence for him as their leader. When he spoke, they hung on to his every word. Srinivas Vadlamani, who was Satyam's chief financial officer, was arrested for his alleged involvement in the scandal. When interrogated, he said that he had tried several times to resist the instructions to commit fraud but that he could not because of a "master–servant relationship" (Timmons 2009).

After Raju disclosed his fraudulent behavior, local shopkeepers, who had previously welcomed Satyam employees with significant discounts, withdrew them. Banks in India canceled the credit cards of the employees (there are few places in the world where this would happen). And in this country where most marriages are still arranged, we witnessed another phenomenon: Engagements and marriage ceremonies were called off. Whereas before, parents whose child was betrothed to someone working at Satyam knew that their child would be marrying a person employed by a highly regarded company, now parents changed their minds. As Ramesh Kuttappan, one person who experienced this, told us, "All of this had an impact on my personal life, too. My family had chosen a woman for me to marry, and her family had agreed to the match. After the crisis, her family changed their minds as they were unsure of my job security."

After the fraud crisis struck Satyam, nonstop information continued to bombard us for days, weeks, and months as the results of accounting forensics were revealed. Over time, the investigation discovered that the fraud, which had originally been tagged at $1.5 billion, was actually closer to $2.5 billion. In addition to the chairman, the managing director (who is Ramalinga Raju's brother, Rama Raju), the chief financial officer, and approximately 10 other senior leaders were charged. With these revelations and indictments, distrust and fear wove their way into the foundation of Satyam's culture.

Four Steps for Shifting the Culture during Turbulence

Turbulence of any kind can affect an organization's culture. To prepare for these changes, the necessary steps to protect and adjust the organizational culture must be planned, and this planning needs to be done before, during, and following turbulent times. This is an area where learning and development professionals play a primary role. Because they have regular access to more people than those in any other part of the organization, they are uniquely prepared to play a powerful role in its revitalization. They can gather information, facilitate learning solutions, communicate changes, assist in determining necessary cultural changes, and provide coaching for leaders to introduce and reinforce desired outcomes.

Moreover, learning and development professionals, given their scope of responsibility, are well positioned to observe the organizational culture as it grows over time. And thus they also tend to be well aware that because people tend to be comfortable with the current organizational culture, for them to consider cultural change, a significant event must usually occur. An event that rocks their world—such as the firm's flirting with bankruptcy, suffering a significant loss of sales and customers, or losing $1 million—might get their attention (Heathfield 2008). This event can be the catalyst for shifting the organizational culture. Even so, attempting to change this culture could well be the most difficult project you will ever take on. To meet this challenge, we recommend that you follow these four steps, which have been tried and tested many times, as you seek to shift your organization's culture:

1. Identify the existing culture of your organization.
2. Proactively influence your organization's culture by facilitating what to keep, what to eliminate, and what to add.
3. Revisit your organization's core purpose and values, and reorganize them if necessary.
4. Communicate and reinforce the core purpose and values.

As stated above, organizational culture includes both conscious and accidental dimensions. A significant change, stemming from either positive or negative forces, presents a unique opportunity to evolve toward a more carefully planned culture. Let's consider how following these four steps can help you guide this evolution.

Step 1: Identifying the Existing Culture

When identifying the existing culture, due consideration should be given to the negative influences that result from fear, anger, and other emotions that might emerge. These should be replaced with positive behaviors and systems that motivate people and enhance performance. The importance of identifying both the written and spoken and also the unwritten and unspoken aspects of the culture cannot be overestimated.

(If your organization merges, is acquired by, or acquires another organization, proper cultural blending is the only way to ensure success. To blend cultures and avoid cultural tensions, you can follow the same four steps being considered here. Make sure the organization's culture aligns with its goals and primary purpose. Tension arises when there is a lack of alignment or when separate cultures are not appropriately blended.)

Step 2: Facilitating What to Keep, What to Eliminate, and What to Add

Once the organization's existing culture has been documented, bring leaders together and decide what to keep, what to eliminate, and what to add to the organizational culture. In making these decisions, the organization's core purpose and values—whose detailed considerations we discuss in the next step—are critically important as the key filter through which each aspect of the culture must pass. In chapter 3, we discussed the advice given to us by global leaders. They told us: "Revisit the core purpose, including core values, vision, and retrospect. Look back at exactly what went wrong, comparing circumstances with the initial vision and values. Identify which actions diverted from them, and build, reinforce, and reestablish values."

A revisited, revised core purpose requires further consideration before it can be implemented. All leaders must choose whether or not to be on board. Those who opt out should negotiate an exit strategy. The upshot from changes in the core purpose that result in a turnover of leaders will be reorganization. There are good reasons for this to happen:

+ It ensures that the leaders who are aligned with newly defined boundaries are the ones who end up leading. This reduces the chances of people feeling that there are favorites who are allowed to remain even if they are not aligned.
+ If the crisis was caused from within, the organization should sanitize itself, removing everyone who was even remotely involved. Unfortunately, this may result in a few innocents being asked to leave; however, the risk/reward trade-off ought to be considered.
+ The organization can add or remove layers of leadership to remove needless complexity and empower leaders.
+ The organization can seek to solidify its resilience.
+ If the organization is involved in a merger, acquisition, or takeover, it can look for ways to integrate leaders from both companies into one unified leadership.

Step 3: Revisiting Your Core Purpose and Values

Regardless of the cause, your organization's core values should be revisited, adjusted, communicated, and reinforced. In his book *Leadership Without Borders*, Ed Cohen (2007) conducted a global survey of 250 senior executives who had lived and worked in more than 60 different countries. The results identified 14 specific core values that are vital for all leaders:

+ *Conviction:* Conveys sincerity and confidence in beliefs and decisions; willingness to make and stand by difficult decisions.
+ *Diversity:* Values different perspectives; builds multifaceted, diverse teams; seeks to understand what drives and motivates individuals.

+ *Entrepreneurship:* Recognizes opportunities and organizes resources to maximize them.
+ *Excellence:* Strives for excellence, which is not the same as perfection; recognizes that "excellence" may vary from country to country, depending on the local context.
+ *Fairness:* Makes decisions that are fair, consistent, and equitable.
+ *Humility:* Acts in the knowledge that he or she is not better or more important than others.
+ *Integrity:* Demonstrates honesty and makes ethical decisions.
+ *Passion:* Leads by example; demonstrates a high level of energy and enthusiasm.
+ *Perseverance:* Shows resolve in moving toward the path that has been laid, with a strong will and the drive to accomplish.
+ *A positive attitude:* Maintains a positive attitude; represents decisions and policies in a positive manner.
+ *Respect:* Demonstrates a high regard for others, regardless of their station in life; treats everyone with dignity.
+ *Service oriented:* Provides extraordinary, "extra-mile" assistance to everyone, whether an employee or a customer.
+ *Teamwork:* Easily adapts to being a team player; encourages teamwork throughout the organization.
+ *Work/life balance:* Balances time spent at work with other dimensions of one's family, community, and social life.

Current organizational environments are filled with people who fear stepping forward to expose issues, concerns, and even potentially risky behaviors. This necessitates the need for an additional core value—courage.

+ *Courage:* This final core value is especially crucial for the times in which we live. It entails being willing to stand up and speak for what you believe is right, even when it is the minority view; being willing to take calculated risks; being willing to learn from mistakes; and being willing to speak the truth, even to those above in the hierarchy.

According to Ira Chaleff (1998), "Lack of courage by those serving senior leaders has contributed to the downfall of many once-powerful leaders. But even in the absence of dramatic topplings, the price organizations or groups pay for lacking the courage and skill to address dysfunctional behavior by leaders is high. You can't have a truly participatory workplace environment if the tough issues get swept under the rug and are only discussed cynically behind the backs of the group's leaders." This underscores the essence of courage as a key core value; everyone, not just leaders, is responsible for their organization's behaviors and outcomes.

Core values represent the essence of who you are and how you behave. Standing by core values in difficult times is the best way for leaders to demonstrate their true character and that of their organization. How profound are the words of Alexander Solzhenitsyn (1978) in *The Gulag Archipelago*: "In keeping silent about evil, in burying it so deep within us that no sign of it appears on the surface, we are implanting it, and it will rise up a thousandfold in the future. When we neither punish nor reproach evildoers, . . . we are ripping the foundations of justice from beneath new generations." Be willing to have difficult conversations, be willing to make difficult decisions, and do not tolerate, under any circumstances, a lack of alignment with core values. Quickly ask people (especially leaders) who make such compromises to leave.

When Satyam's School of Leadership was launched, the firm had no explicitly stated core values. Instead, the *Satyam Way* manual conveyed its values as only "AICS [again, associates, investors, customers, and society] Delight." To assist the firm in fleshing out these values, we applied the results of Ed's research (Cohen 2007), introducing these core values to leaders across Satyam. Most were favorable to our proposal and looked forward to communicating and living these values. However, when we presented them to Ramalinga Raju, he was adamant that the only values the company would ever have would be AICS Delight. This thrust us into a quandary. Knowing that the culture needed to be rooted in core values and that we would not be able to convince him, we sought an acceptable alternative. Without the ability to implement core values, we developed and implemented the concept of a social agreement. Let's briefly examine what's involved in such an agreement.

Developing a Social Agreement

A social agreement is basically an agreed-on "way of working" that provides a clear explanation of the relationship expectations within a work team. These include unwritten and unspoken norms, values, behaviors, and best practices. At Satyam, we conducted workshops with the leaders from each key business area. These leaders, in turn, worked with their teams to develop their own agreements.

A social agreement makes the implicit values and expectations of a team explicit. It creates a way to give feedback and hold individuals accountable, and it allows new members to have a context for how the team works. For instance, in our work with Satyam, the social agreement that was developed for one business function included these points:

1. Adhere to the Satyam Way.
2. Praise in public; coach in private.
3. Demonstrate open and honest communication.
4. Be on time, every time.
5. Maintain confidentiality as requested.
6. Take issues to the source, rather than others.
7. Support and own decisions; be accountable to ourselves and each other.
8. Respect and leverage differences.
9. Be clear on goals, roles, and responsibilities.
10. Collaborate.
11. Celebrate successes large and small.
12. Have fun.

A social agreement is launched as a change initiative in four phases: awareness, adoption, penetration, and measurement. In fact, core values or any other changes in the ecosystem can be rolled out triumphantly if you adhere strictly to the sequential order of these phases. These phases are discussed in detail later in this chapter.

A few words of caution are needed here. In the absence of core values, a social agreement works as a temporary substitute. However, when core values do exist, the agreement should be developed to amplify the values, bring clarity where needed, and articulate the realm of acceptable behaviors.

Rebuilding Trust

There is a saying in Hindi, "Satyameva jayate," which means "truth alone triumphs." If you are transparent and speak the truth at all times, then trust is renewable each and every day. If you have built a trusting relationship with people, they will give you the benefit of the doubt when trouble comes. And of course trust, or the lack of it, is a basic underlying reality for all efforts to revisit your core purpose and values. As we discussed in chapter 3, trust can and must be continuously rebuilt. Here are some guidelines for rebuilding trust:

+ Acknowledge individual and team contributions.
+ Sustain and continue to build strong relationships.
+ Conduct skip-level meetings (that is, meetings for which a leader goes below a level to have a conversation with those who do not report directly to her or him) to enhance approachability.
+ Emphasize collaborative decision making.
+ Choose not to collude in the blame game.
+ End rumors before they start.
+ Help those who become displaced find new positions.
+ Learn to detect and "call out" deception. In *Survival of the Savvy: High-Integrity Political Tactics for Career and Company Success*, Marty Seldman and Rick Brandon (2004) provide excellent information on how to detect deception.

Moreover, your organization can assist leaders so that trust is maintained by choosing to quickly

+ Sanitize or eliminate the leaders who caused the turbulence (if intentional) or have seriously broken the trust.

- Reinforce or launch core values.
- Hold everyone accountable for "cleaning up the mess" and moving forward.
- Close communication gaps that cause breakdowns in trust.
- Provide safe ways for people to express themselves.
- Overcommunicate.
- Conduct a regular trust-indexing exercise (a one-minute survey asking employees about the trust level of their leader, the leader's leader, and the organization's leaders).
- Reward honesty, even when it results in negative business outcomes.
- Explain difficult decisions.
- Quickly and painlessly finalize arrangements for those who must be asked to leave, providing special care and sensitivity for those who are laid off.

When Ramalinga Raju resigned, Satyam was first led by Ram Mynampati, whom everyone suspected was complicit in the fraud. Then the government took over and appointed a board of directors. The new board appointed A.S. Murthy, a long-tenured senior leader in the firm as the interim CEO. They went on to sell the company. Throughout this course of events, everyone remained suspicious. When the new owners, Tech Mahindra, checked in, a few politically savvy leaders remained in the system, even though everyone believed that they had been involved in the fraud. In fact, the company secretary, G. Jayaraman, continued to serve the government-appointed board of directors until 10 months later, when charges were filed against him. Shadows of doubt lingered for more than a year after Satyam witnessed its darkest hour. The power and gift of trust should never be underestimated or shoved aside. As Abraham Lincoln said, "You can fool some of the people all the time, and all of the people some of the time, but you cannot fool all of the people all the time." Without trust, your organization's culture will carry a norm (unwritten and mostly unspoken) of skepticism toward all leaders. Mark Twain said it best: "If you tell the truth, you don't have to remember anything."

Step 4: Communicating and Reinforcing the Core Purpose and Values

With the revisited core purpose in hand, leaders on board or filtered out, and renewed energy, now is the time to properly implement change. At this point, there are a few words of caution to heed, because most change initiatives fail to stick. The reasons:

✦ The organization gives up in midstream.
✦ There are inconsistent messages.
✦ There is a lack of follow-through.
✦ There are attempts to measure the results too soon.

There are four stages that, when followed in exact sequence, drastically boost your odds of implementing and sustaining a successful change initiative:

1. Create awareness.
2. Move quickly to adoption.
3. Penetrate deeply.
4. Implement measurement.

Let's briefly examine each stage.

Create Awareness

The more people who hear of the changes and can describe them, the greater the awareness. So stage 1 in implementing your important changes to core purpose and values is to create awareness. You are marketing the conscious organizational culture, so get creative. Make the updated organizational structure and cultural guidelines known to everyone. Information should be available everywhere—online, in the hallways, in the cafeteria, even in the bathrooms. Meeting agendas ought to contain discussions on the subject of the core purpose. Commence awareness contests and announce daily winners. Hand out fortune cookies with the core purpose in them. Give people caps, shirts, and jackets. Use every opportunity to create awareness. Continuously emphasize the value proposition for the changes. Have leaders conduct sessions with teams to familiarize all and respond to queries. Have an awareness plan that reaches everyone in the shortest period. When we helped Satyam roll out the Full Life-Cycle Leadership model, we conducted 75 live webinars in 60 days that reached more than 95 percent of the firm's 22,000 employees. For consistency, each webinar contained a prerecorded overview of the new model. After the overview, live web sessions with senior leaders allowed employees to gain clarity.

After several weeks of blasting messages, use an online quiz to gauge the level of awareness. Review an aggregate average score rather than individual scores to determine the success of the awareness campaign. Do not count adoption, this comes later. And do not use these scores for any purpose other than gauging awareness; that will come in stage 4, measurement. A common error occurs when you leap from awareness to measurement ahead of adoption and penetration. This is one of the reasons why most change initiatives fail.

Move Quickly to Adoption

It is imperative to move quickly beyond awareness to stage 2 in implementing your change initiative, adoption. Launch small pilot groups. Less formally, observe and broadcast examples of the new core purpose being implemented. Look for the smallest of wins, and enthusiastically celebrate and communicate them to all. By now, leaders should have been trained and be on board with the desired shifts. They must be role models and brand ambassadors of change, reinforcing positive behaviors and coaching those who require added insights. Learning and human resource professionals can assist leaders by facilitating groups and providing individual coaching during this stage. They can seek answers to queries and build a robust intranet portal that answers frequently asked questions. During this stage, persistently refer to the shifts in core purpose, and tie all behavior back to this purpose. Continuously recognize and reward early adopters.

Penetrate Deeply

Once a few visible parts of your organization adopt the updated core purpose and there's relatively broad awareness, it's time for stage 3 in implementing your change initiative: to penetrate deeply into the organization.

Anyone you ask about the core purpose should be able to engage in a dialogue about it. This is the time to continuously remind people about and reinforce best practices and also to make sure that all learning programs—including those for employees and new hires—are infused with the needed information, skills, and behaviors. Moreover, one way to reinforce your overall change initiative is to reward those who are role models by enabling them to teach others about successful practices. If done consistently, over a short period, the excitement this generates will stimulate more adoption. Eventually, most employees will have adopted the new core purpose. However, don't begin the celebrations yet. There is one more critical stage to go to ensure the change is sustainable.

Implement Measurement

You are equipped for moving on to stage 4 of your change initiative, implementing measurement, only when the awareness, adoption, and penetration stages have been sequentially and fully completed. If one stage has not been completed in its entirety, attempting measurement has the potential to result in botched change. Measurement should start with regular feedback and the tracking of progress. This eliminates the surprise reaction that measuring might otherwise cause among employees. At Satyam, for instance, we implemented four ratings: role model, consistent, building, and issues. (These ratings were also used by Booz Allen Hamilton for its assessment ratings.) A 360-degree feedback instrument aligned with the organizational culture allowed everyone to gain a rapid view of how they were perceived. The results were used for giving feedback and for setting actionable goals. Later on, the 360-degree feedback instrument was repeated, and this time the outcomes became a part of an employee's annual appraisal. It is imperative to continue to reward role models publicly. In fact, Booz Allen Hamilton is so serious about its core purpose and values that it presents VIP awards to its role models—with VIP standing for "values in practice." A paid vacation for two, extra time off, spending money, and a beautiful engraved gift come with the honor. Suffice it to say that the rewards are huge. And the firm doesn't just bestow one award a year on one person; it presents dozens of them each quarter. These awards are considered the highest honor an employee can achieve.

Summing Up the Four Steps for Shifting Culture

A crisis or other significant change stemming from either positive or negative forces presents a unique opportunity for guiding the evolution of an organization's culture toward one that is conscious. But having everything well documented is not enough. An implementation plan that includes the four stages (awareness, adoption, penetration, and measurement) discussed in this chapter increases the odds of a successful cultural shift. To recap, these four steps are (1) identify the existing culture of your organization; (2) proactively influence your organization's culture by facilitating what to keep, what to eliminate, and what to add; (3) revisit your organization's core purpose and values, and reorganize them if necessary; and (4) communicate and reinforce the core purpose and values. Once these steps have been completed, success is achieved when the organizational culture has evolved to primarily embody written and spoken norms, behaviors, and practices, and less desirable unspoken and unwritten behaviors have been left behind.

Cultural Mismatches

One final caveat is needed here about cultural mismatches when organizations are facing turbulence. During a turbulent time, the heightened and often-chaotic quest for power results in a situation where some leaders end up with more responsibility and others with less. Talented leaders are lost in the shuffle. This happens most often when cost optimization results in good people being displaced without regard to their existing contributions or prospect for having a positive impact in the future. Even those leaders who are best suited to help the organization through a crisis may be shunted aside. This situation leads to high turnover rates among leaders, which causes constant shifting within the organization as people are realigned and reassigned. This reintroduces fear and uncertainly into the organization's fragile ecosystem. And if these negative norms are not handled with extreme care, they could accidentally turn into part of the organization's new culture. In this context, it is useful to once again turn to Satyam's experience.

On January 18, 2010, the cover of *Businessworld* magazine featured a photo of Anand Mahindra, vice chairman of the Mahindra Group, with the title "Bringing Back Satyam: How Mahindra Is Rebooting Satyam" (Subramaniam 2010). As was mentioned in chapter 3, the Mahindra Group bought the troubled Satyam in April 2009. The article retells the story of what happened from the early days of the crisis to today. In the article, Venkat R. Gajjala, team leader of Integrated Engineering Solutions, recounts that "I had a top MNC [multinational corporation] client with 400 Satyam employees in the US. For employees, with no big bank balances, getting paid on time was a very big worry. We (team leaders) spent a lot of time reassuring them that money would reach them on time."

Later in the article, Anand Mahindra refers to his firm's successful bid for Satyam: "We were like commandos hitting the ground. We had a simple, twofold strategy. First the corporate governance gap had to be plugged. We would do that by walking the talk. Second, and equally important, was to adopt a profit-centric approach to business."

As Mahindra's role at Satyam unfolded, a significant cultural mismatch surfaced. The top priorities of the revived organization were governance and profitability. But what about its employees? The new management team told the employees that the environment would be much more open, yet their actions contradicted this. In chapter 3, we discussed how the most common mistake leaders make during any kind of turbulence is implementing cost optimization without considering retention. The media reveled in reporting that 8,000 employees had been placed on sabbatical and 3,000 had been invited back. However, they neglected to realize that the resulting impact of cost optimization and the perception that employees were not a priority would translate into greater fear and less motivation. Extensive turnover ensued, as nearly 20,000 employees negotiated their exits or moved on. At one point, more than 100 people a day were leaving the company. To slow turnover, Satyam's new leaders needed to quickly move back up the employee relationship chain (see chapter 7), and that would have meant making retention a priority. We discussed this at length with the new managers, but no substantive action was taken. They did reinstate variable bonuses and implement salary increases. They threw a few parties and came up with some creative ideas for contests and how people could dress for work. Yet they did not take the critical steps to reduce fear, rebuild trust, and demonstrate how important employees were to the recovery (as we will explain in detail in chapter 7). This perceived lack of priority for its people thus became an accidental part of the newly revived Mahindra Satyam's organizational culture.

The fundamental message here is to say what you do and do what you say. In the case examined here, to avoid a mass exodus, it was imperative for Mahindra Satyam to balance the priorities of governance, customers, profitability, and employees. Likewise, for any organization's culture, unwaveringly leading through learning, sharing successes, openly communicating, and providing positive reinforcement are tantamount to triumphantly emerging from the gloomy shadows of turbulent times. Clearly, you can see how organizational culture influences everything that happens. As we have shown, it can evolve consciously or by accident, and a conscious culture has a far greater probability of enduring while the organization thrives.

Key Points

Key points for guiding the evolution of your organization's culture during a crisis:

+ In turbulent times, additional norms, behaviors, and practices creep into an organization.
+ Countless leaders do not recognize the influence that organizational culture has on the past, present, and future accomplishments of their enterprise.
+ Every organization develops both a conscious and an accidental culture. Its conscious culture unfolds from its written and spoken goals, values, behaviors, and practices that are taught, measured, and reinforced. Stemming from the unspoken and unwritten, its accidental culture is revealed with seeming randomness over the course of its history.
+ The culture of the geographical region(s) in which an organization has its roots significantly affects its culture.
+ Turbulence of any kind can be the catalyst for shifting the organizational culture. To shift the organization's culture, identify

what exists and then bring leaders together to decide what to keep, what to eliminate, and what to add.

✦ Regardless of the cause of turbulence, your organization's core values should be revisited, adjusted, communicated, and reinforced.

✦ A social agreement is basically an agreed-on way of working that provides a clear explanation of the relationship expectations within a work team.

✦ Without trust, your organization's culture will carry a norm (un-written and mostly unspoken) of skepticism toward all leaders.

✦ With a revised core purpose in hand, leaders on board or filtered out, and renewed energy, you are ready implement change.

5

Coaching for Leaders

✦ ✦ ✦

Smart human capital leaders are quickly discovering
what matters most to those whom they can ill afford
to lose and then providing it.

—Preston Bottger

✦ ✦ ✦

Today, leaders face more demands than in any other time in history. The necessity to collaborate requires a united approach to align with corporate goals and thus have the maximum chance of achieving success. And depending on whether the leader is in the ranks of senior executives, in line for succession, or a relative novice, the path is different for each. More and more successful leaders are turning to coaching. A coach is a trusted partner for a leader. Finding this kind of partnership in an organization is unusual. A coach can give a leader the opportunity to create and safely explore new options and to process what has or hasn't worked. A coach truly vests in the leader's success above all else. Once leaders experience this, they are more receptive to using coaching conversations with their teams. And leaders who clearly experience the value of using a coach as a sounding board are able to easily adapt these newly learned skills in the workplace.

When a company is dealing with significant change and turbulence, coaching is a vital part of the solution. According to Preston Bottger (2009) of the IMD business school in Lausanne, "Investment in human capital must focus on the critical factors in the firm's business system: its products, customers, competitors and internal structures. Leaders are concentrating the efforts of their high-talent people on maintaining cash flow by making and selling products and serving customers. Importantly, they are also finding the best ways to develop their people despite the economic turmoil."

When your organization is facing a significant challenge, you must use every resource available. When resources are slim, coaching is one service that can make a tremendous difference. For instance, when the crisis imploded our world at Satyam, the leaders were left to pick up the pieces. Under the shadows of corporate corruption, the leaders fell into the unenviable position of having to retain and regain the trust of their work teams and customers. But we had a pool of professionally trained coaches, and this gave us a tremendous head start.

During a crisis or other major change, even if your organization does not have professional coaches on staff, its leaders still need to be willing to coach and to be coached to accomplish the organization's turnaround. Not knowing which direction to turn, who they can trust, or to whom they can convey their thoughts and expose their fears, leaders struggle to find a way to balance the growing demands of customers, investors, and even their own team members. Leaders end up being caught between their loyalty to the company, their teams, and their need to protect themselves and families. With these concerns in mind, executive coaching is critical to the learning strategy for enabling leaders to fulfill their roles.

During an organization's period of extreme change, the inevitable terminations, separations, and reductions in workforce strain an already damaged system. Given these widespread challenges, it is not sufficient to only provide leaders with a coach to allay the spreading anxiety, fears, and loss of motivation. With employee retention as a major concern, it becomes essential to have proliferating coaching conversations across the entire enterprise. For Satyam, the investment in coaching had a tremendous impact. Likewise, you need to provide coaching for all leaders and help equip your leaders to provide coaching to others.

In a situation such as the one that Satyam faced, how can leaders handle the massive workloads ahead of them, now doing the work of three others along with their own, until the organization "rights" itself? Leaders will have new challenges, need to welcome unfamiliar team members from other units, find the appropriate fit, and learn the best way to manage new team members. They will need help blending cultures. Employees will be faced with similar challenges. Many will be transferred to new departments or business units with new, unfamiliar leaders.

To further complicate these obvious challenges, the end result may not be clear. In Satyam's situation, we did not know at the beginning whether the organization would be closed, merged, or sold. Leaders needed to be prepared for and armed with tools to achieve rapid and continuous change management. Though additional resources were made available, such as a help line and an intranet portal with answers to frequently asked questions, we recognized all too well that our leaders were clearly in the position to have the greatest impact.

Everyone is required to wear multiple hats when rapid changes are happening. For instance, Satyam's leaders, with the help of the internal coaching community that assisted them with their own challenges, were able to face an onslaught of stress known only to those who have ever had to survive a crisis of this magnitude. As team members came to them for help, they were able to work with them to find solutions, assess the impact, and provide motivational opportunities to assist the company in orchestrating its turnaround.

With this key role for coaching in mind, let's look at the basic steps in developing your organization's coaching function:

+ Provide coaching for *all* leaders.
+ Show concern for all employees.
+ Help leaders have both a macro vision and a micro vision.
+ Reinforce coaching by encouraging connectedness.
+ Select and utilize coaching questions.
+ Start a help line.

Provide Coaching for *All* Leaders

Coaching becomes fundamental when leaders face uncertain times. Skilled internal coaches can go into action immediately to provide a rapid response, and so they must be assigned proactively to all leaders. If the organization does not have these coaches on staff, members of the learning team can be quickly acquainted with coaching approaches and methodology. Powerful, generative questioning techniques are more easily adapted by skillful facilitators. We see this as a more immediate solution in a crisis. Using highly trained and certified internal or external coaches provides more experienced partners for leaders and is preferred, where this option available. Whether the leader is new in the position or has years of experience, none is exempt from struggles during a crisis. Leaders often need more support than others as they design the maps containing the details for charting the company's way through turmoil. Without these maps, the entire organization is without a path to follow. Through the coaching partnership, the leaders are better equipped to identify new approaches and manage the quagmire of challenges ahead. Executive coaches help to provide the necessary catalyst so that leaders can find their internal confidence, discover new approaches, and engage innovative solutions to motivate their teams. Thus, instead of beating their heads against the wall or surrendering to seemingly overwhelming circumstances, leaders are empowered to seek methods to turn around difficult situations.

Coaches reach out to leaders and help by asking powerful questions to challenge their thinking and problem-solving capabilities. They are in regular and frequent contact with their assigned leaders, breathing new life into the coaching relationship and, in turn, the organization.

At Satyam, as the demands on existing coaches grew, we came to the realization that even with our full contingent of available coaches (though these continued to be reduced in number due to cost cutting), we would still be unable to reach all the leaders who needed coaching. Our solution was to equip the leaders with the resources so that they themselves would be able to use coaching approaches with their team members. This process required coaches to prepare their leaders to take on the responsibilities of coaching with their next-level leaders. An enormous advantage of this is that it includes the opportunity to model a coaching approach in a company culture of uncertainties. To accomplish this, coaches begin sessions with leaders by requesting that they become more heavily involved with their team members and others in the organization. Coaches provided new tools to assist leaders in having conversations with those who reported directly to them and with those who reported to those leaders. For one coach's experience, see the sidebar.

Rohan Shahane's Coaching Experience

Rohan Shahane served as the lead for executive coaching at Satyam. He assisted in the deployment of coaching programs. He shared his experience: "As I looked around the organization, I found leaders and business units in some places who, even though bruised and injured, were able to march on. What was happening here? How was this possible? What did it take for them to soldier on? There were many reasons expressed. A sense of commitment and loyalty to the organization, pride in one's work, solid camaraderie among the team, and a deep customer relationship were just a few. However, there was one thing in common that stood out strongly: These leaders were authentic, transparent, and humble. The crisis has thrown up many lessons for all of us, and the one enduring lesson that I take from this experience is what I have begun to call 'fearless authentic leadership.'"

Show Concern for all Employees

In a predicament like the one we faced at Satyam, there are many relationships to rebuild. Unlike most organizations that focus on customers first, we took the position that employees should have equal priority. Within every organization that has been hit by a calamity, there have been talented employees who put aside their fears and returned day after day to reassure customers that all was not lost, that they still mattered. Though a CEO or president can fly around the world to meet with a customer face to face, any employee's true measure of worth lies in his or her daily face-to-face interactions with those with whom they work—and thus there are leaders of morale at all levels. And these leaders need your support. They are the final measure for whether a customer will continue to do business with you.

The best way to send the message that employee retention is paramount is to focus on leaders. Help leaders figure out how to be visible and authentic, demonstrate genuine concern for others, listen, and show empathy. Empathy comes from listening as if the other person is the only one in the world at that moment. Have you ever experienced this?

Help Leaders Have Both a Macro Vision and a Micro Vision

It's important for leaders to have both a macro vision and a micro vision. Good leaders must be capable of being able to see what does not yet exist. They need to have a clear repertoire for market conditions and be a predictor of changes that will affect their organization and the organizations they serve. They must be able to anticipate the challenges of their "stakeholder's stakeholder" and adapt rapidly when change is required; they must embody empathy in the face of adversity, and they must engage in strategic analysis on a par with their client. This is a "macro vision"—what is the future, and how do we get there? This quality is a tremendous gift because it allows leaders to take calculated risks that can have an enormous potential to affect on the organization's profitability and long-term success.

Equally important, and often not given the attention it deserves, is the ability to have a "micro vision." What this means is the ability to not only look beyond where you are now but also to look into the details of the organization's present and history. What are the patterns that have affected us, and how did we get where we are today? A scanning and acknowledgment of signs noted, as well as those missed, indicates that we are where we are today because of the actions of our past and our present. Working with a coach can help bring this to light and help us to evaluate those lessons that will help us steer a new course for the future.

Let's take a simple example of this dual vision. When a leader engages with a few peers on the team and holds them accountable for the remainder of the team, this can be very effective. It saves time, empowers others who may be in line for succession, and can potentially increase the productivity of all involved. Yet much can be lost. By adding weekly team meetings and skip-level meetings (where a leader goes below a level to have a conversation with those who do not report directly to him or her), a leader can create the opportunity for more innovative thinking, while keeping everyone involved in a collaborative approach to finding new and better solutions. When all your leaders are doing this regardless of level, and when all employees are expecting it and asking for it, that's when the organization's leaders are truly united in what the outcomes can be.

Satyam used this approach during its crisis. Coaches assisted leaders in taking both a macro and a micro view of their world. Leaders were encouraged to find out what was going on in their teams—not through those who reported directly to them but by seeking out the individual members of the team and getting to know them better. Leaders were fundamentally advised to get involved with those team members with whom they might have nothing to do on a daily basis—get personal, find out if they were OK, find out if their families were OK, share realities, learn about their fears, tell them what could and couldn't be done, and tell the truth about what, as a leader, they could and couldn't control.

So our recommendation is to tell them how it's affecting you. Be real! Research results indicate that those leaders who get involved with their teams—who truly connect—face fewer challenges in keeping their teams motivated and involved in pursuing the organization's survival.

Reinforce Coaching by Encouraging Connectedness

Employees generally will give everything they have. Those who feel this deep level of connectedness show it to others. As a coach or a coaching leader, you can reinforce this connectedness in multiple ways:

+ Meet with leaders to ensure that they know that expressing their own feelings and fears is appropriate.
+ Let everyone see your strength and commitment to the organization and your struggles to save it.

✦ Acknowledge your pride in having such wonderful team members.

✦ Equip your leaders with additional methods for having conversations and a set of powerful questions to elicit answers. (Sample questions are given below.) These powerful questions reflect the leader's true interest in hearing open and straightforward responses.

Give critical attention to the feedback from your coaching. The template given in table 5-1 provides guidance to help leaders identify coaching goals and review progress and challenges. Although this template is useful for any circumstance, it can prove particularly valuable during a crisis, when leaders need a sounding board and confidante to process decisions more clearly. Using both a coach and one another as peer coaches can be very powerful. Use this template in your coaching conversations, and show leaders how to use it successfully in seeking to answer the key coaching questions, to which we now turn.

Select and Utilize Coaching Questions

When conducting coaching or peer coaching sessions with leaders during turbulent times, there are a number powerful questions from which to select. These questions, which are used in the context of the coaching approach template given in table 5-1, cover the gamut—from the leader, to the team, to both the macro and micro vision with respect to the team, to the customer relationship, to gaining commitment. Let's consider sample questions for each topic.

Here are sample questions about the leader:

✦ What challenges have you identified?
✦ How are you prioritizing your time?
✦ What is needed to make things easier on you?
✦ How are you getting what you need?
✦ How often do you speak with your manager?
✦ When are you scheduled to speak again?
✦ What is your manager telling you?

Table 5-1. A Template for Approaches to Coaching

Leader:	Session No.:	Date:
Coach or peer:	Location:	Time:

Note: This template is a tool that both the coach (peer) and leader can use together each time they meet.

At the beginning of the session, take the necessary time to discuss any challenges that might prevent either leader from committing 100 percent to the designated time. Remind each other that each should ensure they are in a place free from interruptions before starting each session.

Ask powerful questions (see the sample question sets in the text) to elicit where each is at this point and determine the direction of the session.

Refer to this Coaching Approach Plan, agreed upon by both parties, before initiating the coaching relationship, for reviewing goals, approaches, and action steps for this session. Feedback on progress should be specific and timely. For example: "I am clear about my progress because my increased ability to delegate the right task to the right leader has improved delivery time."

Goal	Approach	Action(s)
1.		
2.		
3.		

Progress on Actions / Successes	Leader's Learning / Insights	Actions before Next Session
1.		
2.		
3.		

Explore challenges that could limit the ability to accomplish the identified action steps (see the sample questions in the text on gaining commitment).

_____

_____

_____

Next meeting date, time, and location: _____

+ What additional help do you need from your upstream leaders or from others in the organization?
+ How could additional training, consulting, or coaching be helpful to you at this time?

Here are sample questions about the team—with respect to the macro vision:

+ When was the first time you spoke with the team about the crisis?
+ What did you communicate to them?
+ What haven't you told them? Why?
+ How is the team doing? How are they handling the situation? Do some team members need specific help?
+ When will you speak with them next?
+ How often are you scheduled to update them?
+ What are you planning to tell them the next time you meet?
+ What's on the minds of your team members?
+ What types of communication challenges are you encountering?
+ What kind of help do you need in having some of the more difficult conversations?
+ What actions are you implementing to keep your team members motivated?
+ What are the short- and long-term employee retention plans?

Here are sample questions about the team—with respect to the micro vision:

+ What individual meetings have you had?
+ What are some of the common themes?
+ What are some of the unique concerns?
+ What processes are in place to ensure that every team member has individual meetings with a leader?

Here are sample questions about the customer relationship:

+ When did you last speak with your customers?
+ How have your relationships with your customers been affected by the crisis?

+ What in particular are you doing vis-à-vis your customers to handle the crisis?
+ What are the short- and long-term customer retention plans?
+ How could additional training, consulting, or coaching be helpful to you at this time?
+ What help would you like from others in working with the customer?

Here are sample questions about gaining commitment:

+ When should we speak again?
+ What will you have completed before we next speak?
+ How will you know you have been successful?
+ How much time each day are you willing to set aside to handle these tasks?
+ If you are not successful, what could have gotten in the way?
+ How might you break the action down into smaller, more manageable tasks?
+ Who else needs to be involved for successful completion of the actions?
+ What help is needed to ensure that you are able to complete these tasks?

In considering these questions, keep in mind the day-to-day realities of coaching. In this regard, see the figure on coaching tips and the sidebar on the experiences of Priscilla Nelson.

Start a Help Line

Even with a successful coaching program in place, employees need another outlet—another place to turn. One solution is a help line. Help lines can provide resources in a timely and cost-effective manner. Frequently asked questions can be uploaded onto a readily available online access point, where employees can write in with their additional questions and get immediate answers or referrals to a "live" attendant. Telephone lines can be staffed by trained associates who provide immediate feedback and can assist in assessing the needs of the employee to direct him or her to the appropriate resource.

✦ Coaching Tips ✦

- ✦ Establish trust—build rapport every time you meet.

- ✦ Focus on the person you are coaching—be on time, every time, and listen authentically.

- ✦ Determine one or two goals that are measurable and attainable.

- ✦ Ask powerful questions in a spirit of purposeful inquiry.

- ✦ Don't ask closed-ended questions that can be given just a yes-or-no answer.

- ✦ Have the person identify resources and support systems; assist only if needed.

- ✦ Don't give advice in the form of a question.

- ✦ Create shifts in thinking—ask how else might you achieve this goal.

- ✦ Set action steps, and hold those involved accountable.

- ✦ Empower and motivate, and acknowledge effort.

More details on each of these tips are available at the website for this book (ridingthetiger.com).

The Voice of Priscilla Nelson

I had been providing leadership development and executive coaching for leaders from *Fortune* 500 companies for many years before moving to Hyderabad to work for Satyam. There, my responsibilities included building a global executive coaching program for the company. We began with the most senior leaders and then cascaded coaching throughout the entire organization. From the beginning, it was a formidable venture. The cost of doing business in India was significantly lower than in most countries where Satyam had offices. This factor, and the added factor of the culture's reticence to use external coaches, resulted in our decision to build an internal coaching capability. Building a strong, professionally trained, and competent resource pool of coaches was paramount for our strategy. Further, it was imperative that we meet the needs of our diverse culture. Though mostly of East Indian origin, our customers and onsite employees represented differing national origins, and therefore our coaches needed extensive training in cultural awareness.

When I arrived in India in 2005, I discovered that coaching was not well known there. Most saw coaching as a "remedial" approach for those who were struggling—all but a "last ditch effort," before they were asked to leave the organization, or school, where their success or failure might well determine their destiny. With this kind of a perception, and in the predominantly Indian-centered corporate headquarters, coaching would have a long, uphill battle to be seen as a strong resource for leaders. In one conversation with one of our most senior leaders, we were told, "Yes, I can see this as a tremendous asset; I have some leaders I want to refer to you." Our response was, "That's wonderful, and how could coaching affect your own growth?" By allowing this leader to realize that he could reap value, he was also willing to present himself as a role model and catalyst for others. Taking all this into account, it was apparent that a massive shift in the perception of coaching was required before executive coaching services could be successfully launched.

We developed a two-pronged approach. The first prong involved one-to-one engagements with senior leaders, getting them acquainted with the infinite possibilities for building on the success of a solid career. We began by telling everyone that coaching was for successful leaders; we were not there to "fix" anyone. It started slowly, and over time it began to gather a following. The second prong entailed more comprehensive programs, including "group coaching" programs for new and emerging leaders, and coaching support for those pursuing new leader certificates and global business leadership opportunities. This further embodied the core messages of our coaching relationship: trust, partnership, and accountability. The pipeline for coaching included individual senior leaders; leaders in transition; new leaders, both promoted and hired from outside the organization; and emerging leaders.

To prepare professionals as coaches, we sought the right training. We worked with several external providers and also developed our own internal certification program aligned with the organization's core competencies, as well as the core values and code of ethics of the International Coach Federation. Armed with our new internal program, we groomed a strong contingent of 45 professionally trained coaches who stood ready to match their skills with the needs of our leaders. By 2009, we had the largest internal professional coach program in Asia and quite possibly, the largest in the world. Coaching was the cornerstone of all our professional service offerings. Executive coaching became a critical service, noted in each and every award the organization received between 2006 and 2009. Our coaching model has been used as a baseline by other organizations throughout India as they have created their own coaching programs.

In many organizations, a help line like this can be set up through an additional link on an intranet home page aligned with a standard Employee Assistance Program, which includes referrals to employee assistance counselors and a list of resources and frequently asked questions. A decision is often required to determine whether coaching or counseling is necessary for dealing with stress or, on a deeper level, with depression or anxiety, which may be getting in the way of the employee's daily routine at work and at home. Many of the companies that provide insurance services to employees include five visits before referring a person for more comprehensive care. However, in global corporations, this option is not always available. At Satyam, we implemented a telephone help line and a link from our home page. Those in the United States and Europe used the Employee Assistance Program and online access, while employees in those countries where this option did not exist were provided access to a telephone call-in number and online access.

Here again, coaching was a critical resource. With the safety and well-being of our employees being our first priority, carefully trained screeners made the determination as to whether the caller's challenges could be addressed by internal coaches or if a referral to an outside counselor would be better. All employees placed in the virtual pool were offered the opportunity to work with a coach and participate in group coaching programs. We knew that career planning, designing a résumé, or preparing for an interview is often stressful even in the best of times. Working with coaches outfitted employees with new tools and brought to the forefront their skills, enhancing confidence so as to be ready to apply, interview, and be selected for new positions.

Looking at the Big Picture, and Summing Up

It must be obvious by now that coaching can be the solution for many challenges. Coaching serves as a solid complement for the majority of service offerings, and technical and nontechnical programs alike are served by building powerful questioning into the facilitator's presentation. It is a tested approach for growing leaders and a tested approach for support and continued development of senior leaders and their teams—before, during, and after a crisis.

Most coaches have had the opportunity to form a partnership with at least one leader who has had his or her work/life balance affected by global economic uncertainties. You've heard the phrase "it's lonely at the top." Leaders not only have a vantage point that few others share; they also have few people with whom they can share it. In "Top Dogs Are Lonely: Confessions of a CEO Coach," Ray Williams (2008) writes, "A CEO coach can be a trusted role model, advisor, guide, and mentor who helps the CEO shape visions, tap new energies, and generate desired results. But more than anything, the CEO coach can provide an oasis of calm, relationship of trust, and honesty to help the CEO fulfill an extremely demanding role."

Let's digress for a bit and consider the case of those leaders who were involved in the deception at Satyam. One might speculate that these leaders simply made poor decisions, resulting in Satyam's fall from grace, and that coaching might have made a difference. However, it is our opinion that long-term struggles with integrity far exceed any relationships that even the best coach could have managed. There may be some argument that with early intervention and a strong coaching relationship, those who got caught in the deception might have made different decisions. We may be talking about a very fine line here. Lessons from Enron, Worldcom, and others have demonstrated that many leaders who got caught in the less ethical decisions of others were simply people of high integrity who were unable to stop others from propelling the organization in the wrong direction (Brenner 2009).

It can be a very delicate balance for a coach and one that, as coaches, we must also answer for ourselves before engaging in such a dangerous relationship. Coaches must first and foremost be above reproach and have clarity about the expectations of their clients. Their role is not to judge or condone. They must unswervingly follow a clear code of ethics. So it is indeed a dichotomy for a coach to accept a client for all they are and at the same time for all they can become.

The impact of organizational politics is also important to recognize as both a contributor and deterrent to poor integrity. When we were at Satyam, the co-author of *Survival of the Savvy*, Marty Seldman (2004), came to Hyderabad to meet with our most senior leaders. Seldman told us that organizational politics helps to determine the ultimate success or failure of an organization and that how we view and use these politics could help carve out a leader's career path within an organization. Most of us see politics as a dirty word and try to stay out of it. Yet how we manage the politics of an organization can be either a tremendous asset or a tremendous liability for our personal career growth, innovation, and creativity. If approached with savvy, it can aid us in choosing and building relationships with leaders who come from a place of integrity. And as we were to realize later, how to form partnerships with those same power centers could ensure job protection in a highly volatile market.

Whatever type of coaching relationship you are in, remember that coaching is not about providing the right answer but about using impeccable listening skills to help people find the right answer for themselves. It is about challenging them to reach beyond where they are, to dig deep into their soul for the courage and insight to reach a higher potential than perhaps they had ever considered. Recall the inspiration of Martin Luther King Jr. or Gandhi, and imagine a parent who must find the courage to stretch the limits of a child with disabilities so that he or she can achieve dreams beyond expectations. These individuals reached down into themselves to bring out their best. A coach sets these kinds of expectations. When you use coaching in your work with peers and team members, you become both their strongest advocate and most critical assessor. You must know what they are made of and hold them accountable for the tasks ahead. There are instances where being direct and offering suggestions is appropriate, contrary to many schools of thought in coaching. Many coaches fear that being direct will be misinterpreted as a consulting function, however, and may fail to push their clients to reach their truest potential. Coaching requires you to use myriad tools, yet you must know when to use them. Equip your leaders with the tools they need, and also give them the guidance to use them to achieve success.

Key Points

Key points with respect to coaching for leaders:

+ A coach gives a leader the opportunity to create and safely explore new options and to process what has or hasn't worked.
+ During a crisis, even if your organization does not have professional coaches on staff, its leaders still need to be willing to coach and to be coached to accomplish the organization's turnaround.
+ Skilled internal coaches can go into action immediately to provide a rapid response, so they must be assigned proactively to all leaders.

- If the organization does not have coaches on staff, members of the learning team can be quickly acquainted with coaching approaches and methodology.
- Research results show that those leaders who get involved with their teams—who truly connect—face fewer challenges in keeping their teams motivated and involved in pursuing the organization's survival.
- When conducting coaching or peer coaching sessions with leaders during turbulent times, powerful questions can assist in gaining better clarity and generating options.

6

Using Social Networking Media

✦ ✦ ✦

To say that we are closer to victory today is to believe, in the face of the evidence, the optimists who have been wrong in the past. To suggest we are on the edge of defeat is to yield to unreasonable pessimism. And that's the way it is . . .

—Walter Cronkite, American broadcast journalist

✦ ✦ ✦

Social networking media are becoming more and more important tools in these turbulent times. From relaying the first messages and pictures from the scene of Chesley "Sully" Sullenberger's heroic Hudson River jet plane landing to helping locate survivors of the earthquake in Haiti, easy-to-use and cost-effective technologies such as Twitter have served as indispensable lifelines of communication during catastrophes and crises. At Satyam, Twitter's 140 characters were not enough to keep our massive workforce engaged in the latest news. We needed to act quickly and decisively and find a communication medium that could deliver large amounts of content while also "putting a face" on the situation.

We felt human contact was essential—not just text messages but also a person serving as an advocate. So we started our own news agency. Web video and radio allowed us to be fully transparent and consistent with our Lights On strategy, and so we extended this strategy one step further—to include "Camera, Action!"

Let's visit our show. The TV program's director, Tony Chapman, says "5-4-3-2-1," points, and we are on the air. "Namaste from Planet Satyam," says the host. The camera pans back from the opening signage and zooms in for a close-up of the participants in the studio (figure 6-1). "In this program, we will be discussing how to weather the storm. My guest for today is here to help us to find ways to get through this turbulence."

During a corporate crisis, it is necessary to find a scalable, flexible, and reliable solution to rapidly communicate with everyone around the world. In most cases, you should be able to leverage existing technologies to make this happen. Developing a 24/7 social media presence is within the realm of possibility for any organization. Today, web TV/radio capability is as simple as a Skype or Yahoo connection. A small investment in a high-quality video camera and a media server further extend this capability.

Working in partnership with providers of internal communications, web TV/radio can rapidly become an emergency broadcasting network

Figure 6-1. *Priscilla and Pragnya Seth Host a Talk Show at the Planet Satyam Studio.* (Photograph courtesy of Ed Cohen.)

for organizations facing turbulence. It provides a common place for all to turn for ongoing information and allows learning to continue without interruption. At Satyam, within less than two weeks after the crisis struck, we had ramped up to more than 600 hours of programming a month, all using the existing network infrastructures. For any firm with moderately advanced technical capabilities, web TV/radio, with both live and on-demand programs, can be used to reach employees around the world.

Back in the studio, the show is ending. The director signals and says "3-2-1 and we're out." After a pause, you hear, "Good show everyone." The lights in the studio dim. The team jumps into action, resetting the studio for the next live program, which is set to begin in 5-4-3-2-1. Now let's take a look at how to implement web TV/radio and utilize some of the other social networking tools available to rapidly and regularly reach target audiences.

Implementing Web TV/Radio

You do not need a significant depth of knowledge about technology to make web TV/radio a reality. The technical aspects are actually simple. True quality comes from using a professional camera and high-caliber audio with the right format.

Let's digress and discuss format. *The George Burns and Gracie Allen Show*, which premiered on October 12, 1950, was one of the first comedy series to make the successful transition from radio to television. Similar to the format of the radio program in which George Burns and Gracie Allen played themselves, the CBS domestic comedy was set in their home, the first TV series to depict the home life of a working show business couple (Gibberman 2008). When TV was first introduced to the world, early programs replicated radio broadcasts; announcers and storytellers stood in front of microphones delivering their messages. Luckily for us, however, this new medium of TV provided much more diversity. Sets were added, and people began to move around. The ability to record for later playback allowed directors to do takes and retakes. Along the way, the world began to develop its fascination with talk shows. Around the world, talk show hosts brought guests on to share information, talk about ideas, and pontificate on areas of expertise. See the sidebar for more on web TV.

The Voice of Tony Chapman, Leader, School of Leadership

With more than 20 years of experience in media and television production, I had decided it was time for a change of pace. I joined the School of Leadership at Satyam in March 2008 as a leadership development consultant. I quickly became immersed in the training programs, teaching conflict management tools, tips on executive presence, and presentation skills.

At the end of 2008, my family traveled back to Australia for the Christmas break. On the evening of January 7, I was at a party at my sister-in-law's in a beachside suburb of Melbourne. It was the usual raucous family event, with friends dropping in and wine flowing. In the midst of all this, I decided to ring the office in India. This is how I learned about the massive fraud. I felt a bizarre sense of dislocation, magnified by the distance between my family there and my colleagues in Hyderabad. I imagined what they must be going through and their reactions to this news.

On my return to work a few days later, it was clearly "all hands on the pumps." Faculty and support staff were gearing up for crisis management and morale-sustaining initiatives that could be disseminated to the staff at zero cost. One key communication platform during this time was the webcast studio we had been testing for the past year, known as Planet Satyam. As web television assumed growing importance as a communications tool that could operate on a minimal budget, I was drawn into working in the studio. My plans to develop my skills as a leadership learning professional were put on hold.

We had a number of memorable webcasts, including series such as *Rise of the Phoenix* and *Weathering the Storm*. At the end of January, we ran a five-hour-plus webathon to raise funds for a local orphanage with which we were heavily involved. We had one camera going live and another crew picking up interviews at the back of the webcast area. The enthusiasm of everyone involved carried the day, and we managed to raise a considerable sum.

By the end of October, web television was being used to deploy almost 90 percent of all learning. My desire to be a leadership development professional remained sidelined, so I decided it was time for me to move on.

The point here is that as we have shifted from classroom to virtual delivery of learning, we have, in most cases, attempted to replicate the classroom in a virtual environment. This has resulted in "talking heads" and streaming text and graphics flashing on the screen. However, participants in these programs are not enticed for long, especially when they are at their desks and it is competing with so many other priorities and interruptions. So is there a way to motivate learners to stay?

If we take our lessons from the transition from radio to television and recognize that this new medium has so much diverse potential, then the answer is a resounding yes. However, when web TV/radio capability arose a few years back, we forgot the lessons learned from the early days of television. We repeated history by replicating the meeting rooms, auditoriums, and classrooms in a virtual setting. We failed to provide readily available useful and interesting information. This is how we came to adopt the term "edutainment" and launch a series of learning programs in talk show formats. Using a TV guide format, webcasts and webinars are scheduled, and people are kept informed. In any situation that involves cost optimization, whether a crisis or other operational challenge, travel is usually the first expense to be frozen. Offering learning, with a more informal approach, is the best way to reach a large mass of people with little development time needed.

To achieve this, the right mix of programming needs to be determined. This will depend upon the needs of the business. The right mix of learning attuned to the needs of the target audience is optimal, with a program mix that includes

+ 35 percent for formal learning
+ 35 percent for communication
+ 25 percent for "edutainment"
+ 5 percent for program promotion.

Establishing Key Roles

Venturing into new areas beyond formal learning requires assistance from across the organization. All programming should emulate mainstream live television studio production, meaning it must be professional, predictable, and repeatable. To make this work, there are several key roles, including producer, program owners, program advisory team, technical advisory team, scheduler, program quality consultants, and business analysts.

The *producer* is the primary leader of the studio. This person is responsible for managing the implementation of the vision and must be highly organized and adept at dealing with a multitude of personalities.

The *program owners* are responsible for the identification of learning objectives, topic selection, and securing the right subject matter experts (guests) well in advance. Because learning objectives are normally established for a series, the topics are well defined and identifying experts is simpler. Because guests require little preparation (there are no scripts and definitely no presentations), they are more likely to be willing to participate.

The *program advisory team* is responsible for reviewing all program requests to make sure they meet standards and provide learning on a timely basis to achieve specific business objectives. During times of turbulence, this is paramount. The team consists of the producer, people from learning, and people from other key parts of the organization. Finance, administration, human resources, legal, and customer relations units are some of the areas that should have representation on this team.

The *technical advisory team* should be chaired by a senior member of the IT department. Doing so will provide more leverage than you can imagine when it comes to the continuous creativity and innovation that are required for quick development and success. Other team members include the producer, a leader from finance, and technical experts.

The *scheduler* makes calendar placement decisions, assigning programs to fill slots throughout the week. It was amazing to watch people vying for what they considered the prime time slots.

The *program quality consultant* monitors the quality of the broadcast by checking in with people around the world (similar to an audit) to make sure that it is clear and audible. This is a real-time role. The consultant also assists those individuals who may have difficulty accessing the program signal.

The *business analyst* collects and measures results that are linked directly back to the business.

Developing Learning Sessions

Here are sample guidelines for developing successful learning sessions:

+ Each "talk show" program is 45 minutes.
+ Each program series aligns with a theme. We chose six themes—technical, domain, process, professional development, leadership, information dissemination, and "edutainment."
+ No scripts or presentations are allowed. This does not imply that programs are a free for all. Content owners need to determine learning objectives and sequence to ensure maximum learning and information dissemination. Program owners align objectives with topics and identify the right subject matter experts—that is, guests.
+ Guests are informed of the topic and objectives. They are discouraged from coming to the studio with scripts. Guests can participate from the studio or over the phone.
+ Participants can call in and comment or have their questions answered.
+ Handouts can be downloaded to supplement a program.
+ A three-minute commercial break takes place in the middle of the program, allowing everyone the opportunity to quickly check for timing and make adjustments if required.

Providing Continuous Program Availability

If you need to reach people around the world, the best way is to produce eight hours of live programming per day and then replay it, two more times, in eight-hour blocks. If the capability exists, programs can emanate from anywhere in the world, providing a live experience for everyone.

Within less than 24 hours of Ramalinga Raju's resignation from Satyam, we held an invitation-only, live webcast for all our customers around the world. We were told by our customers that this simple act helped them to feel more confident in our ability to regain our footing. When Tech Mahindra purchased Satyam, we held a company-wide meeting using web TV to broadcast Anand Mahindra, the vice chairman of the Mahindra & Mahindra Group. The live and archived session reached more than 40,000 people. Our crew had to compete for coverage with a multitude of reporters waiting outside. This was a news event across all of corporate India.

Here are some of the many programs we developed for web TV/radio:

+ *Daily News:* Imagine tuning in every day to catch the news of the organization where you can inform, respond to the press (all the things the press says about your organization that may or may not be true), and provide words of wisdom from leaders.

+ *Weathering the Storm:* By addressing the global economic storm and its effects, this daily program provided an opportunity for leaders to hear about how other leaders both inside and outside the company were adjusting and innovating.

+ *The Rise of the Phoenix:* Using case studies provided by Harvard Business School Publishing, this program explored the lessons from other companies that had gone through major turbulence and rebuilt to new levels of success. As with all other programs, *The Rise of the Phoenix* was a 45-minute segment with a case study that was discussed, with lessons learned extrapolated to assist our journey. In *How the Mighty Fall and Why Some Companies Never Give In*, Jim Collins (2009, 24) articulates his rationale for studying the fallen "One of the keys to sustained performance lies in understanding how greatness can be lost. Better to learn from how others fell than to repeat their mistakes out of ignorance." While we agree with Collins that studying how greatness can be lost can be a preventive measure, it is even more vital when a company has fallen and wants to rebuild. Learning from others who have walked the path of destruction and risen again, like the Phoenix, proved to be a solid learning experience (see the sidebar).

The Rise of the Phoenix, by Anil Santhapuri

There is a legend about the mythical bird called the Phoenix. This creature, with a tail of beautiful gold and red plumage, had the distinction of transforming itself, every 500 or 1,000 years, by burning up fiercely and later rising as a young, newly transformed Phoenix.

Every organization encounters turbulence at one time or another. Many do not survive. A select few organizations not only survive but utilize turbulence as an opportunity to rise like the Phoenix. There is much to learn from their stories, which is why we chose to develop this topic into a web TV program when we were faced with our turbulence. Over a two-month period, we reviewed and discussed eight case studies and discovered eight common themes that translated into tasks:

1. *Revisit the core purpose:* It is paramount to assess if turbulence has emerged due to misalignment with the core purpose and values of the organization. For example, in 1982, when Tylenol was poisoned by cyanide, Johnson & Johnson responded by reemphasizing its values—integrity, customer safety, and product quality—and thus recalled thousands of bottles. Though this meant $100 million in damages, it actually helped restore Johnson & Johnson's credibility and serves as a classic example of how to respond during what could have been deadly turbulence (Augustine 2000).

2. *Focus on employee confidence:* Most leaders involved in turnarounds cite rebuilding the confidence of employees as their top priority. In some cases, tough measures must be taken, such as letting employees go. Remember this important message from Gordon Bethune, CEO of Continental Airlines: "People want to be led, not managed, in a crisis."

3. *Engage key stakeholders:* First, identify all key stakeholders, then immediately reach out with relevant messages. Leaving behind some of the stakeholders or not spending enough time with them could lead to issues of trust. In the case of the Tylenol poisoning, Johnson & Johnson modeled the way by reaching out not only to stakeholders—but also to the media, employees, the general public, government, and medical professionals—in the spirit that "we're all in this together" (Adubato 2008). In similar situations, then,

leaders need to conduct floor meetings, open their doors, and seek other forms of continuous communication with employees and customers. At IBM, the CEO, Lou Gerstner (2003), announced Operation Bear Hug, to enable senior leaders to visit top customers.

4. *Pursue a proactive communication strategy:* Being proactive includes communicating the right information, at the right time, to the right audience—and even communicating that you have no information. At Cadbury India, when worms were found in chocolate bars, the firm immediately set up a media desk and made sure no query went unanswered (Vaid 2006), which helped to rapidly restore credibility (Phani Madhav and Umashanker 2004).

5. *Take a visible leadership role:* The true test of leadership strength comes during turbulent times. The physical presence of leaders providing regular communication makes a difference, because people look to their leaders for answers and guidance. An excellent example of visible leadership was New York City mayor Rudy Giuliani after the 9/11 terrorist attacks—he immediately reached the scene and then relentlessly led the response (Riley and Smith 2003).

6. *Ensure focused execution:* There needs to be precise clarity in roles and responsibilities for everyone, so that exactly the right things are done at just the right time. Tyco International split its leadership into three groups, each focusing on separate aspects of day-to-day operations, investigations, and customer focus (Khurana and Weber 2008). The focused leader, with the team's help, should identify and take the immediate correct actions. To prepare for this kind of a careful response, many companies develop 30-, 60-, and 90-day scenario plans (see chapter 2).

7. *Rebuild the brand:* This is critical to let people know the organization is back in action with renewed commitment and passion. After its encounter with the worms in chocolate bars, Cadbury introduced secure packaging and aired TV testimonials by a well-known brand ambassador—the Bollywood film actor Amitabh Bachchan (PRCAI 1994).

8. *Keep a sense of urgency:* The scarcest resource during turbulent times is time. Swift and immediate action must be taken to begin putting the organization back on track. Themes

1 through 7 here need to be completed with a great sense of urgency—at the same time. Gordon Bethune calls this "Do it now, right away, and all at once" (Brenneman 1998).

History is witness to organizations that have risen like the Phoenix because they stood up to challenges without giving up or giving in.

With 80 percent of our workforce requiring technical skills continuously updated and upgraded, daily programs like *Tech Talk*, *Let's Talk Project Management*, and *Domain Speak* addressed topics of high interest for the techies. Participants could mail their queries to a designated address, and they would be answered by the panel during the show. Leaders and experts called into the program by dialing through a phone "bridge," so there were no constraints on the quality of discussion. Handouts were downloaded from a shared website. Assignments were completed and returned to instructors (that is, the program hosts) for evaluation.

Another major part of the organization requiring continuous learning are those employees in sales and customer relations. The global economic meltdown, in late 2008, had made things difficult for them. Now, with the organization in survival mode, managing customer demands and expectations was all the more challenging. The learning agenda included programs such as *Business Acumen Round Table*, *Customer-Centric Corporation*, and *Customer Retention Tips*, as well as various best practices, models, and case studies on nurturing relationships and growing a business against all odds.

Programs for friends and family can be broadcast during evenings and weekends. At Satyam, this proved especially valuable for employees who were trying to figure out how to balance the needs of an organization facing peril and the needs of a worried family.

After January 2009, with a total freeze on travel, Satyam's learning delivery was almost completely shifted to the virtual mode. Web TV was able to reach an average of 110,000 (nonunique) participants every month. The talk show format, combined with assignments and coaching, allowed for rapid migration of instructor-led course content to create virtual learning assets that reached thousands of unique users.

Measuring Impact

To measure impact, first measure viewership. Soon, however, end-of-program evaluations (a pop-up window when the participant exits the program) should be added. Later activities requiring participants to complete deliverables to demonstrate the knowledge gained from a series can be added. Ultimately, more sophisticated types of evaluation methods can be used to measure effectiveness and impact.

Open and Honest Communication

At Satyam, daily editions of *News Today Live*, along with live webcasts of employee communication shows like *U Speak*, *Ask Your Leader*, *Surf the Board*, *Direct from the Leadership*, and *Direct from the Media*, contributed to more than 300 hours of communication programming in webcast and webinar formats every month that attracted an average participation of more than 200,000 (nonunique) employees.

Email

Email, that simple tool we have all come to take for granted, is still a powerful and useful medium to assist with the most major emotional concern of affected employees—fear! This is done by sensitizing leaders to the need for constant communication and being available continuously for employees who need to reach out. At Satyam, from the start of the turbulence, we were inarguably the most visible people in the organization, reaching out to communicate and providing information as it became available. You won't have all the answers. Even so, do not duck for cover. Run email campaigns that evoke hope, resilience, togetherness, and passion. This will guide, humor, and motivate a distraught workforce and its equally shattered leadership.

Additional Social Networking Tools

In today's globalized organization armed with publicly available social networking tools, LinkedIn, Facebook, Plaxo, MySpace, and many other sites can be used to link people together. Many companies are engaging in a debate as to whether or not to encourage these tools in the workplace.

It's too late! Around the world, people are using these tools, linking to one another and openly communicating their thoughts and feelings. Rather than discourage this, you should provide employees with guidelines for professional behavior. Setting and communicating these guidelines encourages appropriate usage while providing employees with many more vehicles for communication.

In the wake of Satyam's fraud revelations, websites sprang up everywhere. Rebuild Satyam, Unsung Heroes of January 7, and many more independent and social networking sites were launched. We couldn't stop them, and neither can you stop similar sites. We chose to communicate guidelines and monitor the sites. And these sites ended up proving to be a tremendous source of healing for the corporate masses and a tremendous source of information for us. By actively monitoring them and participating, you can correct misinformation and at the same time learn what people have on their minds.

Key Points

Key points for using social networking media during a crisis:

+ During a corporate crisis, a scalable, flexible, and reliable solution to rapidly communicate with everyone around the world is necessary.
+ Working in partnership with internal communications, web TV/radio can rapidly become an emergency broadcasting network for organizations facing turbulence.
+ You do not need a significant depth of knowledge about technology to make web TV/radio a reality. The technical aspects are actually simpler than imagined.
+ Offering learning, with a more informal approach, is the best way to reach a large mass of people with little development time needed.
+ The right mix of learning is optimal, with a program mix that includes 35 percent formal learning, 35 percent communication, 25 percent "edutainment," and 5 percent program promotion.
+ Sophisticated types of evaluation tools can be applied to measure effectiveness and impact.

✦ It is critical to assist with the major emotional concern of affected employees—fear! This is partially accomplished through sensitive, continuous, communications.

✦ Rather than discourage the use of social networking tools, provide employees with guidelines for professional behavior.

✦ Actively monitoring and participating in social networking can be leveraged to correct misinformation and at the same time enable you to learn what people have on their minds.

7

Caring for the Wounded

✦ ✦ ✦

*We are not imprisoned by our circumstances, our
setbacks, our history, our mistakes, or even staggering
defeats along the way. We are freed by our choices.*

—Jim Collins, *How the Mighty Fall*

✦ ✦ ✦

The media does a fine job of presenting a firsthand view of the after-math of catastrophes caused by weather, natural disasters, wars, and other tragedies. Unidentified bodies lying across ruins, the wounded yet to be counted, heroes carrying victims to safety—these are all horrible sights conjured up by well-meaning journalists. In more recent years, the media has attempted to provide a view into the aftermath of corporate turbulence caused by greed and a lack of integrity. However, they have not been as successful in showing the depths of those wounds.

When a company is in crisis, its employees are always affected. These people work very hard to help fulfill the corporate mission. They range from newly hired graduates to those with 5, 10, 20, or more years of service. And then there are the people who work for the company's primary suppliers. These people have built their businesses based on the company's success. Then, in an instant, this successful company crashes—the greed of a few robbing these loyal employees and suppliers of their futures. What do they do? Where do they go? What happens to their lives, to their homes, to their families? As India's *Economic Times* reported on January 27, 2009, "amid the entire drama unfolding ever since the former Satyam chairman Ramalinga Raju admitted to financial fraud, some Satyam employees feel that everybody from government to investors are ignoring the emotional trauma thousands of Satyam professionals could be experiencing."

So what would have happened if Raju had climbed off the tiger? Would he have been eaten? While he was riding the tiger, did he realize that he was taking everyone with him? When he climbed off, he proved it was possible to do so *without being eaten*. However, it was not possible to climb off without being injured. All connected to Satyam suffered significant wounds. The media referred to all that happened as the "Satyam scam" rather than the "Raju and a few of his colleagues scam." Tainted, disgraced, shamed, beleaguered, and shocked, the vast majority of the people revealed their solidarity and desire to move forward toward rebuilding the company. When a possible purchaser, Tech Mahindra, showed interest in the company, everyone remained optimistic that there would be a rapid turnaround. Even so, everyone grieved. People experienced the full range of reactions:

+ Disbelief, anger, self-preservation, depression, and acceptance took longer for some than others. No leader wants to be responsible for ending someone's job.
+ Those left behind struggled with survivors' guilt, wondering why their friends had lost their positions when they hadn't.
+ Those who remained had to wear the hats of three or four people and faced continuing uncertainty about their future and the prospects of an unknown job market.
+ Some people felt less worthy because they were reduced to reporting to new managers appointed over them when the company was acquired. Some no longer felt needed or valued. Many left the organization, still struggling with their emotional wounds.

✦ Across the board, people were sleep deprived, worried, fearful, angry, shamed, and defamed—not sure which direction to turn, with so many unanswered questions.

In his book *A Sense of Urgency*, John Kotter (2008, 23) explains that "anxiety and anger drive behavior that can be highly energetic—which is why people mistake false for true urgency. But the energy from anger and anxiety can easily create activity, not productivity, and sometimes very destructive activity." During an organizational crisis, there is a paradoxical opportunity to convert emotions into productive action. Leaders must quickly emerge from the abyss to care for the wounded. These leaders need continuous learning to maximize the prospects for rebuilding the organization—assuming they are not the leaders who were involved in the deception that caused the predicament, in which case they need something more than learning.

Most risk-mitigation plans do not consider people's emotional needs. They should. Downsizing is critical to the organization's survival when fiduciary responsibilities are imposed for rebuilding, and risk mitigation involves so much more than that. What steps can an organization take during turbulence to ensure that the emotional needs of its people are still met? Shockwaves of uncertainty, indecision, and worker confusion result in dangerous levels of fatigue and exaggeration. Rumors abound, which can cripple the organization even further. With trust at an all time low, one employee's natural response might be to roll-up her sleeves to keep moving forward. Another might vent frustrations and spread the latest rumor, feeding the already-low morale. And another might simply decide to get out as quickly as possible. When caring for the wounded, keep in mind these three vital considerations:

✦ Communication is crucial.
✦ Everyone passes through the stages of grief.
✦ Employee retention comes from moving up the relationship chain.

Let's take a look at each consideration in more depth.

Communication Is Crucial

As we discussed in chapter 3, even when there is not much to say, there is much to say. Let's put that another way. There will be times when you have very little new information. The urge will be to say nothing until more information is known. This, however, is not the right thing to do. During a crisis, information should be repeated over and over again. People will move through various modes of listening, and as a leader, you are responsible for making sure that everyone has all the information available—whether new or not. Let's briefly look at a number of ways to do this.

Communicate Often

Say what you know and say what you don't know. Do not hypothesize or give your personal opinion about anything. As information comes available, first validate its accuracy. If its correctness is confirmed, then communicate it. If it isn't confirmed, also communicate that. The rumor engine will be spinning at maximum speed, and these actions will hopefully slow it down. Tell people that unless they hear the news from one of the organization's leaders, they should assume that it is only an unfounded rumor. And before spreading rumors, they should check their validity.

Schedule Updates

Scheduling updates provides structure and helps allay fears. If your crisis is born out of an "event," as ours was at Satyam, updates should be provided hourly on the day the news hits. On the first day, schedule updates every hour and provide them whether or not new information is available. From day two through the end of the first week, twice-daily updates should be given (and more, if critical information comes available). From there, you can decrease the frequency of updates. If your crisis is less extreme, biweekly or weekly updates might be more appropriate from the start. People will feel less edgy knowing when and where updates will happen. We conducted webcasts with simultaneous telephone conferencing to ensure that everyone was able to participate. Never cancel an update. If you cannot do it, designate a backup.

Reinforce Messages

Send out notes about every update for those who could not attend. These messages should indicate what was said and all the questions asked and answered. They should also reinforce what was said to those who attended the update.

Meet One to One

You should meet one to one with those who report directly to you and have them do the same with their direct reports. Many leaders will get so involved in the business of the business that they will neglect this. Do not allow this to happen. Require everyone to maintain a log of their schedules. When meeting with leaders, ask with whom they have and have not met. Monitor this closely, because these one-to-one meetings go a long way toward regaining the share of heart (see the section on the relationship chain later in this chapter).

Do Not Chain Yourself to Your Desk

It is imperative that leaders be seen. Do not chain yourself to your desk. Get out and speak with people. Your presence alone will be reassuring. Block out time on your schedule throughout the day to allow open periods to walk around and see how everyone is doing.

Strategically Leverage the Rumor Mill

No matter how hard you try, no matter how many times you tell people not to listen to rumors, they will still exist. If you know the key people who tend to spread rumors, then strategically leak messages to them. Watch and wait to see how fast the rumor goes full circle and back to your door. In other words, one way to slow down the rumor mill is to fill it with facts (covertly and strategically).

Communicate a New Path, a New Vision, and New Roles

During the crisis at Satyam, when we surveyed our LinkedIn contacts from around the world, they said it is important to establish and communicate a new path, a new vision, and new roles for the organization so that people will see the value in continuing rather than being tempted to jump ship at the first chance they get. In addition, they advised that the reinforcement of core values, solid governance, and allowing an open environment where people can voice their thoughts helps further the journey, encouraging employees to regain their share of heart, and promoting steady employee retention.

Everyone Passes through the Five Stages of Grief

During a crisis, all our concentration and energy tend to go into trying to understand the how and the what. How could this have happened? What impact will this have on us? An observable by-product is extreme stress, which very quickly manifests itself as grief. Elisabeth Kübler-Ross (2007) developed an excellent model of grief for death and bereavement counseling, and dealing with personal change and trauma, that we believe is also valuable during times of extreme organizational turbulence. Her model describes five stages of grief:

1. shock and denial
2. anger and betrayal
3. bargaining
4. depression
5. acceptance.

Let's take a look at each of these stages and some of the ways for getting through them with integrity.

Stage 1: Shock and Denial

The first stage of grieving, shock and denial, helps us to survive the loss. In this stage, the world becomes meaningless and overwhelming (Kübler-Ross 2007). It's like being frozen in disbelief. When will I wake up and find out this was just a bad dream? You question whether it's really happening.

When the Satyam scandal broke, everyone went into a state of shock and disbelief. The *Deccan Chronicle*, a regional newspaper, reported that "fear and shock seems to the dominant emotions ruling Satyam employees' minds. 'We are shocked beyond words. We were always inspired by the ethical and impressive demeanor of Mr. Ramalinga Raju. This new development has left us in a state of fear. We don't know what the company's fate will be. We might all just lose our jobs and in the current economic situation, we don't even have prospects of a job anywhere else,' says a Satyam employee."

Leaders, staff concerned with human resources, and learning professionals must heal faster than everyone else. There are wounded for whom to care. Your help is needed, not in a "we are your saviors" kind of way but in a humanitarian way. Reach out individually and en masse. You must be among the first responders. Like all first responders, you must also find time to tend your own wounds. It is important to plan time for self-care. The impact of turbulence affects us all differently. You must be careful to give yourself the required time to go through all five stages of grief, with shock and denial being only the first.

Stage 2: Anger and Betrayal

Anil Santhapuri shared, "My initial shock shifted to anger. We had been cheated. To the outside world, we were all suspects. The media referred to it as the 'Satyam scam.' Within days, many quit and others started to look for new jobs. People were looking for something to hold onto as the trust pillars collapsed. Nothing would be the same again." Underneath anger is pain—your pain. It is natural to feel deserted and abandoned; yes, we live in a world that fears anger. Anger is strength, and it can be an anchor, giving temporary structure to the nothingness of loss (Kübler-Ross 2007). The feelings of being victimized are insurmountable. You want to strike back. Yet you don't know who or where, or even how you will find the energy. During this stage, every ounce of energy seems to be consumed by anger and feelings of betrayal. Nishi Levitt, who moved to Hyderabad in 2006 with her husband and small child, shared this about the anger that grew within her: "How ironic that 'trust' became the epitome of my life as well as the 53,000 employees around me and their families. In one fell swoop it was all over! We were all cheated by a darkened individual who dashed all our hopes. My initial tears of disbelief melded into welts of anger. What now? Where to? I didn't realize I, too, was now riding the tiger. As I write this, the resilience I thought I had built up crumbles."

Nishi left Satyam and has been evaluating and reevaluating the situation to keep herself motivated. Though she recognizes that "things will never be the same again," she also knows that the kind of "same" from before, although unknown to us, was not what any of us would wish for again. By acknowledging her anger and betrayal, she is using these emotions as a catalyst to keep moving forward, an appropriate healing step. Many of us envisage a mental fantasy about how we might get even, take revenge, or punish the guilty. Unless acted upon, this is a perfectly natural response.

Stage 3: Bargaining

The "if onlys" cause us to find fault in ourselves and what we "think" we could have done differently. We may even bargain with the pain. We will do anything not to feel the pain of this loss. We remain in the past, trying to negotiate our way out of the hurt (Kübler-Ross 2007). Employees think of very creative ways to save their jobs—among them, mass salary cuts. Satyam employees, en masse, signed petitions sent to senior leaders recommending a temporary pay cut to keep their positions. There were a variety of offers: reduced salaries, one month without pay, an employee takeover (purchase of the company). Each was an attempt to make use of bargaining to get through this stage. Others are more subtle. They use hope as their bargaining chip. Venkata Subender was one: "The day I was told I was to be let go, I accepted it with honor on the outside. Deep inside, I was in agony. Even so, I held on to the hope that the company would turn around and I would be called to resume my position."

Stage 4: Depression

After attempting to bargain our way through, our attention moves squarely into the present. Empty feelings present themselves, and grief enters our lives on a deeper level, deeper than we ever imagined. This fourth, depressive stage feels as though it will last forever (Kübler-Ross 2007). This stage varies with different people. Some suffer mild forms of depression, while others slip into a deeper depression, inhibiting day-to-day activities. If not recognized and dealt with, this stage can have disastrous results. In one such case an employee working at Satyam in Chennai, fearing losing his job, committed suicide.

This is not a typical response to stress. However, most of us do struggle with varying levels of depression, and fortunately most of us come out of it on the other side. Pragnya Seth understands this well: "Ten months, later in November 2009, as Priscilla Nelson and I were presenting 'Learning Strategies during Turbulent Times' at the International Leadership Association Conference in Prague, I realized my wounds had still not healed. They were still raw, and I was feeling very low. There are thousands upon thousands like me who still feel this terrible pain and sadness."

Sometimes mild depression runs its course and there is no need for follow-up. In other situations, depression can be much more serious. Your response should be setting up a hotline telephone service for those with questions and concerns. Make routine referrals to internal coaches or professionally trained counselors, whichever is most appropriate (see chapter 5 on coaching). Coaches should not provide counseling, yet they should assist with queries, such as

> *What if I lose my position?*
> *How will I find the funds to provide for my family?*
> *How do I tell my spouse and parents?*
> *What can I do if this leaves a black mark on my record?*

Those answering the phones need to be trained in listening. If there are doubts about any employees' ability to take care of themselves or concerns about them hurting themselves or others, they should be immediately referred to professional counselors.

Stage 5: Acceptance

Depression makes way for the fifth and final stage, acceptance. Acceptance is often confused with the notion of being "all right" or "OK" with what has happened. This is not the case. We will never like this reality or make it OK, but eventually we accept it (Kübler-Ross 2007). Kishore Goud, who left Satyam to join another organization in November 2009 says, "Even today the crisis haunts me. Whenever I come across big numbers and large statistics, I get scared and wonder if this is truth or another scandal in the making?" Anil Santhapuri, who chose to remain with Satyam until March 2010, shares, "I fluctuated between discomfort and discovery— sometimes nostalgic of the past, still cautious of the future, my wounds slowly healing."

This final stage happens at different times for different people. Finding some sense of purpose or meaning can assist here. No one will ever know why Ramalinga Raju got on the tiger in the first place. Once on the tiger, why didn't he climb off until it was too late? In their outstanding children's book *Riding the Tiger*, Eve Bunting and David Frampton (2001, 22) provide some meaning. They use a tiger as a metaphor to teach about the powerful allure of gangs. Their main character, Danny, is invited by the tiger to take a ride. While riding the tiger, Danny at first feels great pride and acceptance. But after riding the tiger for a while, he feels bad about his involvement and wants to climb off: "I brought my leg up so I could slip down the tiger's side. 'Don't even think about it,' the tiger said, and when he turned, I saw the yellow glitter of his eyes. I eased my leg back to where it had been before. He was walking faster now and the ground seemed further away." During the acceptance stage, we are more receptive to finding purpose and meaning in obvious and not-so-obvious places.

In the context of our particular experience, "Life beyond Satyam" is the battle cry for many. They have continued to connect with one another. They have remained tethered, always checking in to be certain that all are OK. A special bond was created by our shared wounds. Nicola Klein, who hails from Germany and spent a year in India, told us, "One of my greatest lessons was, if you have a great team of people, working together, who are passionately involved, you can make miracles happen. Having people work efficiently as a team is not easy. It takes a great deal of leadership. When I think of this amazing team, I know 'nobody wins unless everyone wins!' And, we all 'won' by going through this together."

As part of our journey of "moving on" from Satyam toward acceptance, we created a time capsule, which requires a footlocker or trunk and memories supplied by everyone. You can do this with a group suffering from a similar crisis. Gather in a circle and share thoughts about those things of which you are most proud as well as your fondest memories. Have each person bring a physical memory that might include photos, shirts, mementos, and other materials. As each person shares their memories and hopes for the future, the items are placed in the time capsule. In our case, rather than bury the capsule, we entrusted it to one of our team members, who accepted the responsibility for keeping it safe. We all agreed to meet in 2014 to open the time capsule, not as a reminder of the sadness and loss, but rather to celebrate our continuing journeys. In *The Alchemist*, Paulo Coelho, writes, "Everything on earth is being continuously transformed, because the earth is alive . . . and it has a soul. We are part of that soul, so we rarely recognize that it is working for us." Acceptance can come from something as simple as knowing that we will all meet again.

Summing Up the Five Stages

Recognizing the five stages of grief, understanding each, and realizing the wounded pass through them is important to communicate to leaders during turbulent times. Providing ways to observe and detect each stage assists leaders, in real time, as they help the wounded to heal. Armed with this knowledge and guided by coaches, leaders can do more for each person because they realize that the dynamics and experiences of each person are unique.

Employee Retention Comes from Moving Up the Relationship Chain

Moving up the "relationship chain" is critical for organizations. This chain essentially means that effective relations between an organization and its employees (it works for customers with amazing results) leads to a relatively permanent chain, a progressively deepening relationship that endures. A long-lasting relationship that converts to strong retention among employees and customers is the desired result for companies that want to sustain themselves through good times and bad. During a crisis, the relationship is reset or reversed, and you must work to fix it. The relationship chain has three stages:

1. Share of opportunity—contract.
2. Share of mind—partnership.
3. Share of heart—relationship.

These stages have been studied and utilized extensively in the world of marketing and branding, referring to external customers. But they have equal if not greater value in the internal organizational world of employee retention. Let's take a closer look at each stage.

Stage 1: Share of Opportunity—Contract

When a company makes an offer that is accepted by a future employee, many call it entering a relationship. This is not the case. It is a mere contract at this point, not a relationship by any measure. What has just been gained is a "share of the opportunity" for both the company and the employee. Your employee has entrusted the company with the task of providing meaningful work in a secure environment. There is still a degree of skepticism, however, so employee orientation is conducted to assist with the transition. Every now and then, the discussion will be about fit, task, and measures for success. The focus is on adherence.

The vocabulary of the employee also gives you an indication as to the stage you are at. If you are in the opportunity—contract stage, the employee is likely to say, "Tell me what to do. Tell me how I am going to be measured."

Stage 2: Share of Mind—Partnership

In the share of mind—partnership stage, the employee has experienced consistency and decided that there is a fit. This generally happens within the first few months on the job. This stage is achieved only if you have engagement where the company delivers what is promised, especially in the way of meaningful work, compensation, and measurement. You have the employee's share of mind where his or her skepticism turns to confidence. At that time, the employee engages in areas beyond the scope of the specific work assignments. They may join task teams or participate in employee forums and events. The focus at this stage is on the outcome; with less emphasis on adherence (although not less important, as confidence can be lost faster than gained).

This second stage also witnesses a change in the employees' vocabulary, where "Tell me what to do" makes way for "Let's explore ways to accomplish this" and "Tell me how I am going to be measured" makes way for "Help me continue to grow my career."

Stage 3: Share of Heart—Relationship

The share of heart—relationship stage is the most desirable state of the employee relationship chain. Employees view the organization and its leaders as trusted advisers. Now that the company has a share of his or her heart, both are gaining the maximum value, and the employee becomes a true brand ambassador for the organization. Employees share and embrace the organization's vision, core values, and direction for the future. The focus on this stage will not be so much about performing but on transformative opportunities and a deep, sustained impact for both employee and employer (still, the previous two stages cannot be forgotten, for these stages are cumulative). At this stage, if the employee is uncertain about certain aspects of the business, he or she will trust the company to provide the missing pieces. Here, everyone has the opportunity to co-create value. At this stage, the vocabulary of the employee will truly reflect a long-term, sustainable relationship: "We can do this. Let's build a plan for the future."

Why all this effort? It's simple. Organizations witness systematic geometric progression in the retention of their top performers by moving up the relationship chain. This means that if the initial tenure in the share of opportunity—contact stage was X, the second stage could result in 2X tenure, and the third stage could result in 4X tenure.

A Crisis Reverses the Relationship Chain

When an organization faces a crisis, every part of its business is affected, and most revert back to stage 1 of the relationship chain: share of opportunity. How can leaders motivate their people to recommit their talents, energies, and spirit to rebuild the organization? How can the organization move back up the relationship chain to regain stage 3, share of heart? At Satyam, when we discovered that our revenues were not what we had been told, we immediately knew we had too many people and that one of the cost optimization measures would eventually require us to have many people leave. We implemented strict cost optimization measures.

With most employees feeling weathered, hurt, and stressed out, and with their trust diminished, many employee relationships reverted to stage 1, share of opportunity. So how does an organization move back up the relationship chain after it has slipped backward? First, a retention strategy that quickly shifts people from "fright and flight" back to share of opportunity is tantamount to the future success of the organization. This can only happen once the organization is sanitized. This means that all the people, processes, and other support systems that allowed the calamity to occur have been identified and eliminated, with gaps systematically closed. Sanitizing the organization is a very visible way for it to rebuild credibility. People need to see and believe that the organization will not allow the people, processes, and systems that caused or enabled the crisis to continue. Even one exception to this risks the company's ability to move back up the relationship chain.

So, then, shift your attention to identifying and keeping the right people from leaving the organization. According to Preston Bottger (2009), "To begin with, smart executives show talented people that they are valued and spell out the reasons why they should stay where they are rather than move on. And, while bonuses are limited by the economic environment, effective leaders are finding other ways to motivate their people. In this emergency, smart human capital leaders are quickly discovering what matters most to those whom they cannot afford to lose—and providing it." What are the needs of employees in turbulent times? Some critical needs are listed here, in alphabetical order (your priorities will be determined by the requirements of your unique circumstances):

+ assistance with emotional factors
+ consistent decision making about employee policies
+ continuous communication from leaders
+ job security
+ knowledge that leaders value their contributions
+ meaningful work assignments
+ news before it is in the news
+ opportunities to express oneself with leaders
+ patience
+ promotions continuing as planned
+ regular updates on the health of the business
+ reinforcement of core values

+ restoration of compensation (particularly bonuses and variable pay)
+ socialization activities
+ trusting environment
+ understand the way forward
+ workload balancing.

All these are important. Employees want to know they are appreciated. They want to know the organization is stabilizing. They want to see daily signs of improvement. They want a trusting and transparent environment where the news of the day is not something they first read in the newspaper or see on television. They want the news to be communicated rapidly. Access to leaders is critical. Leaders who do not reach out to their people are doing irreparable damage and should not be tolerated.

Recapturing Share of Heart Stabilizes Retention

The best way to determine what employees want is to ask them. In his book *A Sense of Urgency*, John Kotter (2008, 84) tells us, "The idea is simple. Send out 'scouts' who, when they return, bring new information about the world and a new-found determination to do something about the information." Because many will be reticent to voice their opinions in a turbulent environment, online surveys are a useful approach. One-to-one meetings with leaders are also highly encouraged to show they care.

Employees never want to be told that they are less important than customers or shareholders. This is a common mistake for companies experiencing turbulence. They tend to forget that the equation for success includes all stakeholders and that all are equally important. They immediately implement cost optimization measures and customer retention measures. Conversations center on shareholder retention, customer retention, and reputation. They expect more from people who are not displaced, and they expect people to come to work each day with renewed energy. This is not possible! If the organization demonstrates that its priorities are (1) customers and shareholders, (2) cost optimization, and finally (3) employees—its employees will not forget this treatment. This will not result in renewed share of heart. Employees need to know their retention is as important to the organization as customer retention. Of course, it may not be possible to retain everyone. That said, demonstrating priority for employees confirms that the company is engaging in a share of heart relationship that will make the reality of the situation easier for people to understand and to accept.

Once lost, recapturing share of heart is very complicated, much more so than moving from share of opportunity to share of mind. In *Love 'Em or Lose 'Em*, Beverly Kaye and Sharon Jordan-Evans (2008, 305) tell us, "Talent-focused mangers are truth tellers and feedback providers. They do it in a way that is honest and respectful. Preserving the dignity of the other person greatly matters to these managers."

Karl Dumas (2009) provides six lessons for building share of heart with customers that also apply directly to establishing or rebuilding share of heart with employees:

1. Become a student of your customer (in our situation, the employee).
2. Care about what they care about.
3. Give something up.
4. Make fun a priority.
5. Practice generosity.
6. Serve them with extraordinary humility.

Trust is foremost. Employees need to believe their leaders. The ecosystem must not tolerate any lack of integrity or breaks in trust. Even one break will prevent the organization from regaining share of heart.

Key Points

Key points in caring for the wounded:

+ Disbelief, anger, self-preservation, depression, and acceptance take longer for some than others.
+ Transparency and open communication must not only be promoted; they must be sincere and real.
+ Most risk-mitigation plans do not consider the emotional needs of the people. They should.
+ Communication is crucial.

+ Communicate often.
+ Schedule updates.
+ Reinforce messages.
+ Meet one to one.
+ Do not chain yourself to your desk.
+ Strategically leverage the rumor mill.
+ Communicate a new path, a new vision, and new roles.
+ Elisabeth Kübler-Ross's five-stage model of grief is valuable during a corporate crisis: In stage 1, there is grieving, shock, and denial. In stage 2, anger is strength and it can be an anchor, giving temporary structure to the nothingness of loss. In stage 3, people will bargain to try to salvage or get back what has been lost. In stage 4, depression, a sense of loss sets in. In stage 5, acceptance emerges.
+ Employee retention comes from moving up the three stages of the relationship chain: stage 1 is share of opportunity—contract, stage 2 is share of mind—partnership, and stage 3 is share of heart—relationship.
+ A corporate crisis affects every part of the business, in most cases reversing the relationship chain.
+ Once lost, recapturing share of heart is very complicated.
+ Trust is foremost. Employees need to believe their leaders.

8

Salvaging Customer Relationships Through Real-Time Learning

✦ ✦ ✦

Tirelessly develop your reputation for integrity and honesty, and it will become one of your biggest assets as a professional.

—Jagdeth Sheth and Andrew Sobel, *Clients for Life*

✦ ✦ ✦

A corporate crisis of any kind puts a strain on customer relationships. Customers' reactions range from providing a show of faith for the organization to having questions that need answering to deciding to end their relationship. Time is essential. Armed with the tools explained in this book, you can leverage learning and development services to salvage customer relationships.

Once a crisis strikes, innovative approaches are required given the increased complexity employees face along with the lack of time available to dedicate to formal learning. When these innovative approaches are implemented as part of a customer retention plan, they can significantly solidify credibility and relationships. During a corporate crisis, when margins are shrinking and time is precious, customers need to be salvaged as quickly as possible. Here's how you can help salvage customer relationships through real-time learning:

+ Reach out to customers: At Satyam, for instance, within 24 hours of the announcement of the corporate fraud, we leveraged our web television capability to do a broadcast exclusively for customers. During the session, the firm's leaders were able to present and hear from the customers. Use whatever means you have at your disposal, from Facebook and Twitter messages to personal calls to your best customers.

+ When leaders are assigned to coaches, they gain the advantage of talking through their situations as they plan their strategy (see chapter 5).

+ Short, continuously available learning programs have rapid and maximum reach. These programs should focus on best practices for communicating with customers as well as providing the information that leaders need to communicate with their customers.

+ Using real-time learning, you can blend business consulting, organizational development, and both formal and informal training to get to the essence of the crisis and co-create sustainable solutions.

With the primary goal of enhancing customer relationships, real-time learning provides a solid platform for development. It is a leader-oriented, team-customized, consultant-driven, diagnostic-based learning service. Essentially, then, real-time learning includes a needs assessment, consulting, coaching and facilitation, and measurement—all the pillars of excellent learning. The process is based on action research, adult learning, performance consulting, and executive coaching concepts. It is the fusion of development and consulting methodologies. Real-time learning is unique in that there is no single, predefined, frozen content downloaded to an entire group of participants; rather, it is an organic process emerging from the business ecosystem.

With this approach, information reviewed before engagement is combined with observations of and feedback from all stakeholders, including customers. Without frozen content, what drives the program is its *process* and the consultants' skills in observation, feedback, coaching, and consulting, as well as their tool kit of ready-to-use content on a variety of topics, including project management, communications, conflict resolution, and relationship building. The real-time learning process involves three stages (figure 8-1):

1. Collect data.
2. Ignite change onsite.
3. Sustain change.

During these three stages, learning happens on the job, in real time—through a preengagement analysis of information, observation, ongoing feedback, personal development meetings, coaching, team sessions, and extensive follow-up. This process responds to the needs of the business in the "here and now," which is why is it especially vital during difficult times. Let's take a closer look at each of the three stages.

Stage 1: Collect Data

At the outset of the real-time learning process, a performance consultant, who plays a key role in collecting data, is assigned to a customer account.

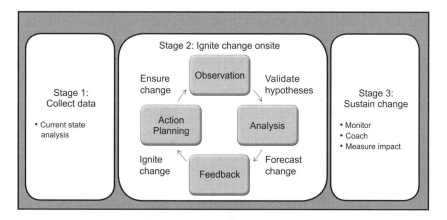

Figure 8-1. *The Three Stages of the Real-Time Learning Process*

He or she meets with the internal business leaders for this account to conduct the initial data gathering. These performance consultants are highly experienced and skilled in consulting, coaching, and facilitation skills. While collecting data, the performance consultant spends time reviewing a variety of inputs and takes time to study the "business of the business" so he or she can have informed and discerning conversations with the leaders of the business area. As the performance consultant studies the business, he or she may conduct the following activities:

+ Review the customer's business metrics for the past two quarters.
+ Study the customer's current projects, revenue, employees, and technologies.
+ Analyze information about the customer's business, its industry, and market trends.
+ Study the customer's employee satisfaction and customer satisfaction surveys.
+ Interview the customer's leaders and as well as their account leaders to get their perspectives on the current and desired states of the relationship.

During this part of the process, a senior performance consultant may be partnered with junior consultants with little or no field experience; these new consultants spend their first engagement observing, learning, and testing their abilities in a safe way. Because the consultants will work with an account or business area for an extended period, relationship-building skills are paramount. See the sidebar for one consultant's experience with real-time learning.

+ + +

Joshua Craver's Real-Time Learning Experience

As a designer of the real-time learning process and a performance consultant based at Satyam, I participated in one engagement that epitomized this type of learning. The members of an onsite account team from Satyam were working with a large customer—a *Fortune* 100 company—with which they wanted to improve their relationship.

Satyam's account leaders wanted our help as performance consultants in meeting two goals: first, to enable Satyam to grow from being the customer's core partner to being its strategic partner—meaning more opportunities for project wins; and second, to improve Satyam's score on the customer's satisfaction survey from 3.67 to more than 4.0 on a 5.0-point scale.

While collecting data during stage 1 of this real-time learning process, we learned that for the past two quarters, this account team had seen increasing revenue but not won any new projects and that the annual attrition rate for Satyam's onsite team was nearing 20 percent. The team identified an increasing threat from other service providers and informed us that there would be projects worth millions up for bid in the next six months. Though the customer was continuing its healthy growth and dominance of its industry, its external perception in the marketplace was not stable. For instance, during one visit we had to make our way through a crowd of protesters upset about its perceived lack of ecofriendly practices.

Armed with extensive data from stage 1, we began to ignite change onsite, stage 2 of the real-time learning process. We started the week with a dinner for Satyam's employees and their families. This helped us get to know the team on a personal level and build trust which would be necessary for our work together. During this week-long stage, we spoke with 18 of the customer's managers, had development conversations with 26 of our onsite employees, and observed 16 meetings. We found that Satyam's employee turnover was essentially due to a lack of cultural integration with the new country where they had been asked to move (mostly from India) and a lack of customer integration. We provided 12 learning and development sessions, all outside billable hours. Throughout the week, observed the Satyam team and customer interactions to ensure that behavioral change was happening, and we ended the week with an action planning session for all stakeholders. This customer employed four vendors with similar capabilities and remarked that our learning and development services differentiated us from our competition. The customer saw this engagement as enhancing its communication and working relationship with the Satyam team, which was previously as roadblock to a true partnership.

During stage 3 of the real-time learning process, sustaining change, we began with writing and socializing the final report. This final report documented all aspects of the engagement. We documented all stakeholders' initial goals, feedback, and thoughts. In addition, we prepared our analysis of the account's current state and opportunities for team development, which included an action plan to strengthen the relationship and business development. From this point we had weekly coaching sessions with Satyam's onsite team leaders, monthly follow-up meetings with the onsite task force, and conversations with key customers to monitor the team's progress. As a result of this engagement, Satyam's team reached its goals outlined from the start. It achieved strategic partner status and a satisfaction rating well above 4.0 during the next customer satisfaction survey, thus well positioning the team for business development.

When the Satyam debacle occurred, we coached Satyam's key team leaders for this customer's account on how to manage the customer relationship and their teams during the crisis. We, as performance consultants, became trusted advisors to the Satyam team—and the team achieved the same status with the customer. Today, this customer is still using Satyam's services.

An important aspect of the process is for the performance consultants to communicate the aspects of real-time learning to all involved—including leaders, employees, and customers—establishing the ground rules for the engagement. This also sets the scope for the expectations of results, so that people will realize that the purpose of this process is to seek ways to improve performance rather than coming in to assess, grade, and punish nonperformance. Making clear what is going to happen and the expected outcomes builds buy-in and trust.

The performance consultants continue to thoroughly review all information available for the business area. This includes review meetings with leaders and finance professionals to understand the financial history and projections for the business area. The consultants also review employee satisfaction surveys, turnover statistics, customer satisfaction surveys, and account plans. The purpose of this step is to gain a broad understanding of the account and to begin to map strengths, weaknesses, opportunities, and threats—known as a SWOT analysis. During this step, the consultants interview key leaders to capture desired outcomes for themselves, for the future, and for the organization, as well as to baseline and establish goals. The consultants concentrate on identifying areas to explore further when the onsite engagement begins. With all the possible information available in hand, major customer relationship themes are identified, and the performance consultants move on to stage 2.

Stage 2: Ignite Change Onsite

After agreeing with project leaders on the most important areas, the performance consultants spend up to a week onsite at the customer's location. During this onsite engagement, the consultants observe interactions between the leaders and their teams and the leaders and their customers. They monitor and probe to uncover performance success and obstacles. Extensive information about the team collected before the onsite engagement contributes to the consultants' ability to quickly assess and assist.

Once uncovered, successes are reinforced and challenges are addressed through pointed learning solutions. Responding in real time to development opportunities the onsite account team and customer's staff face increases the pragmatic nature of the engagement, significantly enhances employee engagement, and prompts immediate behavioral changes. Participants receive feedback and practical tools in the learning sessions that are short and aligned to the day-to-day realities of the job. Moreover, these short sessions do not affect project work or timelines because they generally happen before or after business hours. Sessions fully leverage the knowledge that is in the room and provide guidance to help the team follow through on action items. After the session, the onsite consultant continues observing and giving real-time feedback on the staff's job performance.

The onsite engagement concludes with a meeting attended by the leader, performance consultants, and customer. During this session, the results of the engagement are shared and everyone agrees on an action plan. The customers are likely to be impressed with the time and investment, and the engagement almost always results in a more solid and mutually beneficial relationship.

Stage 3: Sustain Change

After the onsite engagement, the performance consultants develop a final report, which is used to document the account's history, measure the changes that take place, and monitor enhanced customer engagement. The consultants then act as conduits for all the moving parts of the organization. For instance, if financial concerns arose during stage 2, that information is conveyed to that department; if human resources issues were uncovered, they are communicated to that department; and this process continues until the people in all parts of the organization understand the needs of the onsite customer-facing team. Real-time learning is therefore much more than a learning service; it is a true consulting methodology that generates system solutions using real-time data from the teams and customers.

Coaching sessions are scheduled at a minimum of once a week for key leaders within an account team. The sessions' goals are to review action items, discuss the relationship with the customer, and continue to provide guidance to enhance the retention of both employees and the customer. During the coaching session (generally conducted via a phone call), the performance consultants ask a series of questions to generate thought and discussion, such as

+ What is the range from where you are and where you need to be for this area?
+ What are some of the ways you think you can enhance this?
+ How else could you . . . ?
+ When will you know you have achieved this?
+ What's needed for you to achieve success in this area?
+ Where can you get help, ideas, and answers?
+ How will you track and demonstrate progress?
+ What concerns do you have?
+ If you are not successful, what might have gotten in the way?
+ What are the top three goals you will use to measure your success?

These conversations are fruitful for both the leader and the organization. For example, there are instances where direct follow-up with the customer is needed. This should be done only under the guidance of the leader responsible for the customer relationship and generally happens when third party facilitation of a situation is needed.

During onsite work at the customer's location, the performance consultants report directly to key leaders. At the end of the onsite engagement, the consultants work with leaders and the team to develop a solid action plan for the future. Once this plan is agreed upon, the consultants and the team co-create a diverse task force and end the engagement's onsite phase. After communicating reports and the development of the action plan, the consultants routinely follow up with the team to check on progress. Identified measures and metrics are monitored to calculate improvement. Key areas to measure are

+ employee satisfaction and retention
+ customer satisfaction and retention
+ quality
+ cycle time
+ contract renewals or extensions.

By the end of 2008, Satyam's performance consultants had completed real-time learning engagements for 70 *Fortune* 500 customers around the world. Hence, when the firm's crisis hit, we already had established relationships with account teams and customers.

In the days and weeks that followed the onset of the crisis, the leadership consultants reached out to leaders in critical relationship management roles, offering postcrisis guidance and development services. In addition, the consultants contacted relationship managers and collected information that was used to assess and implement solutions during the crisis. We looked at these key areas:

+ the impact of the relationship on customers
+ the impact of the relationship on employees
+ key challenges
+ best practices that the account team had in place for dealing with the crisis that could be shared with account teams.

Real-time learning proved to be a highly beneficial delivery methodology to help leaders rebuild the customer and employee confidence that had been lost due to the unfortunate events befalling Satyam. We were able to use this methodology to enhance productivity and relationships, without taking employees away from the workplace. Of most critical significance, leaders credited the enhanced engagement with customers for having salvaged their accounts.

Key Points

Key points for salvaging customer relationships through real-time learning:

+ Real-time learning is a leader-oriented, team-customized, consultant-driven, diagnostic-based learning service. The process is a fusion of action research, adult learning, performance consulting, and executive coaching concepts.
+ Use real-time learning to monitor and shift relationships.
+ The real-time learning process involves three stages: collect data, ignite change onsite, and sustain change.
+ Real-time learning is a cost-effective and business-aligned learning service that builds credibility with diverse stakeholders.
+ Real-time learning is a highly beneficial process that helps leaders rebuild customer and employee confidence.

9

Leading Through Learning: Creating a Postcrisis Plan

✦ ✦ ✦

*Vision without action is a dream. Action without
vision is simply passing the time. Action with vision
is making a positive difference.*

—Joel Barker

✦ ✦ ✦

During the first 90 days of an organization's crisis or other period of major change, the focus is on keeping the organization alive and moving from one day to the next. That's why the Lights On strategy delineated in chapter 2 is a critical first step. From Lights On, we moved on to guidance for leading through learning in turbulent times, detailed in chapters 3 and 4, followed by coaching for leaders, explained in chapter 5. Then, in chapter 6, we showed how social networking media, specifically web TV/radio, can assist during times of extreme turbulence. In chapter 7, we considered caring for the wounded, and in chapter 8, we covered real-time responses for salvaging customer relationships.

For all the techniques described throughout the book, continuous alignment and retention—of both customers and employees—have been shown to be critical desired outcomes to measure. According to Jim Collins (2009, 117), "The path to recovery lies first and foremost in returning to sound management practices and rigorous strategic thinking." The next step, essentially, is to create a longer-term, postcrisis plan.

In following the techniques laid out in chapters 2 through 8, you've managed to help stabilize the company for the moment. Now it's time to look toward the future. Beyond the first 90 days, you'll need to develop and implement a more cohesive plan, which looks ahead one quarter to one year. This plan includes potential paths for aligning with ongoing business needs, considerations of organizational changes, service offerings, budget allocations, and a solid retention strategy. It's definitely time to get back to this longer-term view. But what do we mean by longer term? During turbulence, "long term" can mean anywhere from three months to one year. See the sidebar for key questions to consider.

Key Questions for Longer-Term Planning

+ How will your business area align with a smaller and more consolidated business with a much smaller team?
+ Who are the key leaders in the organization, and how will your people get to know them?
+ What is the organization's current view of your business area (the past is in the past)?
+ What is the budget allocated, and how will be it prioritized/distributed?
+ How can your business area help rebuild or establish a new brand for the organization?
+ How can your business area be leveraged for customer and employee retention?
+ How can your business area assist with transition to new leadership?
+ How can your business area assist in revving up the sales engine?
+ How will the lessons learned be captured and used for leaders to prevent the same issue from recurring and to maximize strengths?

As the crisis-weakened yet now-stabilized organization continues to deploy services to meet its needs, now it's time for a more future-focused view. The future cannot exist without the past, which is why information about the experiences of all those involved remains critical. There are three primary contributions most valuable to the organization at this point:

+ Be a "partner in change."
+ Conduct a leadership audit.
+ Develop a risk-mitigation plan for the future.

Let's examine each contribution more closely.

Being a Partner in Change

Along with human resources, marketing, and learning and development, your team needs to be well prepared to be a "partner in change" in cooperation with the organization's leaders. This "change" to which we are referring includes cultural shifts, policies, branding—everything that goes into transforming the business and putting it back on the path of success. Your goal is to help align learning efforts with other organizational initiatives that will have the greatest effect on the bottom line. This may include creating learning plans for your team. The need to meet with employees, customers, investors, and other stakeholders is a perfect opportunity to reinforce executive presence, with leaders giving and receiving feedback, and to hone listening skills. When aligned with specific business needs, learning cannot be pushed to the back. It remains on the front line, always providing a real-time response to needs.

As the organization moves back to a more steady state, its leaders need to extend their responsibilities to include being change communicators, change agents, and brand ambassadors representing the shifts required to successfully get through the turbulence. Their priorities thus should be

+ communicating a new/updated vision for the organization
+ strengthening employee relationships
+ reinforcing customer relationships
+ outlining sales competencies

+ identifying functional competencies
+ redefining the roles of leaders
+ identifying leadership competencies for the new environment
+ strengthening the leadership pipeline.

Conducting a Leadership Audit

Strengths, development, and strategies for leadership exist within every organization. However, many do not take the time to pull it all together into one central repository. A leadership audit is an evaluation that is intended to document and expand awareness about the organization's leadership ecosystem. This audit examines the organization's current state of leadership from the perspective of its strengths and limitations. It determines the capacity of leadership and allows for setting a solid plan for the future. Though the value of having this report before any threat of organizational crisis or other major change is obvious, it is imperative after a corporate crisis. The consolidated information it contains is valuable for alignment during leadership transitions, changes in ownership, or points in time as a reference for developing an executive strategy. Use this report to

+ document the framework and current state of the organization's leadership
+ develop a strategy for leadership that is customized to fit the organizational culture, customer focus, and delivery of products and services
+ brand leadership as a strategic differentiator
+ create awareness for new leaders so that their transition to the organization is made easier
+ transition to new owners (which was the case with Satyam).

Similar to the information safari discussed in chapter 2, the leadership audit requires information from all stakeholders as well as existing organizational documents. Because a leadership audit ascertains the strength of leadership and its preparedness for what is happening at that moment in time, we recommend that rather than gathering the data for it from new sources, you gather the data from existing sources, including

+ the company business model
+ statements of the organization's short- and long-term goals
+ interviews with leaders
+ focus groups of employees
+ feedback from customers and suppliers
+ the existing performance management process
+ a leadership survey.

The audit looks at three dimensions of leadership:

+ The leader as an individual, which involves reviewing appraisals and feedback from multiple sources that are mapped to the organization's goals and critical needs to determine how each is doing.
+ The leader's organizational role, which involves examining perceptions of the organization's leadership to identify strengths and gaps.
+ Institutional leadership, which involves examining the tools provided by the enterprise and the influence that the organizational culture has on leadership in its entirety, to recommend systemic changes that would enhance the organization's success and strengthen its leadership.

The leadership audit report is divided into sections on the theory of leadership and the practice of leadership.

The Theory of Leadership

Once all the information for the leadership audit report has been compiled, the leadership ecosystem is identified in one section of the report; this ecosystem includes historical influences (people, process, technologies, markets), cultural concept of leadership, the unique value of the organization's leadership, present influences (people, process, technologies, markets), and future shifts (people, process, technologies, markets).

In this section of the report, leadership roles are codified and examined based on existing performance measures as compared with global research on leadership (for example, as done by Cohen 2007), thereby providing a rapid comparative analysis and recommendations as they are related to the specific circumstance. The strengths of leaders are documented. For us, when at Satyam, this was an easy process. Many of our leaders had completed the Gallup Strengths Finder and participated in coaching sessions. We used the aggregate data for the report, comparing the strengths required to push through the turbulence with the strengths that were already in place. This section of the report should help readers understand how prepared leaders are to lead the company through significant changes. The leadership support infrastructure is documented. What are the existing tools and resources available to help leaders lead? Are these tools being utilized? How do leaders maximize their available resources?

The Practice of Leadership

The section of the leadership audit report on the practice of leadership is based on the perceptions of stakeholders, opinions on facets of leadership, individual attributes, and a SWOT analysis—strengths, weaknesses, opportunities, and threats. The perspective of stakeholders tells a lot about the current state of leadership. There can be plenty of processes and ways of measurement; however, if leaders are not perceived to be modeling the way, this will come to light when asking people about their perception of leadership. This section of the report includes a summary of

+ leader perceptions of leadership
+ employee perceptions of leadership
+ customer perceptions of leadership
+ society's perceptions of leadership.

Two Models of Leadership

One final caveat is needed about leadership audits. In many organizations, there are two leadership models—the explicit and the implicit. The explicit model includes all the written and spoken protocols for leadership. The implicit model consists of the unwritten and unspoken protocols. As part of the leadership audit, the consultant should be able to recommend ways to merge them together. At Satyam, Hetzel Folden, who led the strategic deals practice, observed that he "experienced two types of leadership working in tandem. The first was primarily patriarchal leadership, with agendas and actions controlled by the founder and contrary views summarily squelched. And the second was leadership with high-quality leaders who were globally savvy and worked collaboratively to bring about success to the organization. Out of necessity, these two paradigms of leadership, while sometimes confusing and frustrating, actually worked together."

Utilizing the Leadership Audit—and the Succession Plan

Information from the leadership audit is used to build a robust leadership development framework, which includes

+ a role-by-role, level-by-level documentation of leaders' roles and responsibilities
+ core competencies documented by role and level
+ development factors, including formal learning, informal learning, job experiences, coaching
+ success factors, documented from those who have successfully taken the journey
+ career "derailers": those things that interfere with success
+ colleagues who play informal and formal roles
+ the experiential/work stretch, which includes job rotations
+ developmental assignments allowing for development outside the scope of normal work assignments (that is, task teams, corporate social responsibility)
+ formal training and education to enable competency development
+ recommendations for how the organization can enhance leadership processes and build a stronger pipeline
+ necessary shifts to the organizational culture to encourage the development of leaders who are in sync with each other and the times
+ recommendations for succession planning.

Along with the audit, all critical leadership roles are clearly identified. For each role, a plan is developed for replacing that leader. During a crisis, there will unavoidably be turnover. Leadership roles must be filled rapidly and effectively to avoid weakening the ecosystem. Learning and development play an important role here by helping to make sure that leaders are identified for individual and multiple roles. Coaching for all leaders is imperative (see chapter 5) and must be one of the top priorities in the learning strategy. If new leaders are put in place, learning and development must again step in with the right framework to ensure success.

Developing a Risk-Mitigation Plan for the Future

At several points in this book, we have mentioned the importance of a risk-mitigation plan that includes learning and development. We call this the "Leading Through Learning in Crisis Plan," and it is not one that should be thought up on the fly as you go. As we have learned, when an organization faces a crisis, there is much to do, and gaining agreement proactively before a crisis makes the implementation of a plan much clearer and easier. For each component identified here, you should calculate the cost to implement and also set priorities—while allowing them to be flexible in keeping with the circumstances. The following components that we have discussed in this book should be detailed in your Leading Through Learning in Crisis Plan:

- the Lights On strategy
- communication
- guidelines for leaders
- the culture of the organization and the world surrounding it
- coaching
- social networking
- caring for the wounded
- retention, of both employees and customers
- salvaging customer relationships
- assessing the strength of leadership—the leadership audit.

In the preceding pages, we have presented many tools to help organizations in crisis. We have also provided information shared by the leaders of organizations around the world. Throughout, you have been able to read about the people involved and their experiences. Ramalinga Raju proved that you can climb off the tiger without being eaten—but not without everyone connected being wounded. He rode the tiger at the start of a dangerous, winding, and twisting path that will be traveled by many for years to come. Ramesh Kuttappan put it best: "Sometimes I think of 'going back' to where I was before Satyam. That's when my inner voice takes over, 'Don't go back. Go forward. Be a leader.'"

Key Points

Key points for leading through learning and creating a longer-term, post-crisis plan:

✦ Beyond the first 90 days, it's definitely time to get back to a longer-term strategy.

✦ It is important to know who are the organization's key leaders and to devise a plan for how the learning staff can get to know them.

✦ Leaders need to acquaint themselves with the offerings available through learning services. Whether during turbulent times or not, these resources equip employees with the tools necessary to improve productivity and lead with integrity.

✦ As a "partner in change," assist in enhancing sales skills, employee engagement, and relationships with customers.

✦ By conducting a leadership audit, you will identify strengths and gaps, enabling you to develop a plan to sustain leadership.

✦ The leadership audit examines the organization's current state of leadership from the perspective of its framework and capabilities, considering both theory and practice.

✦ Along with the leadership audit, all critical leadership roles should be clearly identified.

✦ Leaders must rebuild trust with transparency and openness.

Appendix A:
The Legacy of Learning at Satyam

Ramalinga Raju and a small group of colleagues founded Satyam Computer Services in 1987 (you can download the detailed story, "Satyam Computer Services—Becoming a Global Company," at our website ridingthetiger.com). Though most companies grew primarily on domestic revenues, Satyam had emerged as a global company, with most of its revenues coming from outside India. Since 1995, Satyam had focused on addressing the learning needs of the organization through its dedicated Satyam Learning Center. The learning center was located on 120 acres of prime property outside Hyderabad. It sat away from the hustle, bustle, and noise of the city, at the Satyam Technology Center. With state-of-the-art learning facilities—including classroom buildings, a conference center, and onsite dormitories—the learning center was capable of concurrently training thousands of employees a month. Adding to its uniqueness was an outdoor aviary with hundreds of birds, including magnificent white peacocks; a deer park; walking trails; swimming pool; a nine-hole golf course; tennis courts; game rooms; and an amphitheater for outdoor movies and concerts.

Even with such an incredible facility, to meet the needs of the globally disbursed population, close to 70 percent of all learning was deployed virtually. From technology to professional development and family learning, there were extensive opportunities to develop across the company.

In 2005, Ramalinga Raju announced a focus on leadership and innovation in an attempt to turn Satyam's traditional hierarchical organization upside down. The company's leaders believed that to grow faster (they were already documenting greater than 30 percent growth each year), Satyam needed to become an organization where leaders could work autonomously and collaboratively, with greater speed and agility. The central focus was to transform the company by creating such leaders. Satyam's learning offices thus told the world that they were now in the business of creating leaders. So the concept of Full Life-Cycle leadership was developed, whereby the company was divided into logical parts. Each was called a Full Life-Cycle business. They were managed as separate entities that were both independent and interdependent. Ramalinga Raju believed that the Full Life-Cycle leadership model would channel the firm's entrepreneurial energies more effectively. The Satyam leadership implemented the model with zeal, and the results were phenomenal. From 2005 to 2009, the company more than doubled in size.

Launching the School of Leadership

The launch of Satyam School of Leadership in November 2005 and the Full Life-Cycle leadership framework were firm steps that came about as part of the company's goal to strengthen leadership. The school focused on grooming and growing leaders to extend the leadership pipeline. The strategic intent behind the school's evolution was to create an establishment that engendered global business leadership—leaders responsive in real time, who are consistent in making decisions that would delight stakeholders, who were action oriented, and who had the ability to work collaboratively in a networked environment. In designing the School of Leadership, Satyam built an enduring institution that researched and developed opportunities to nurture best-in-class global entrepreneurial leaders. Their first study, in partnership with ASTD, looked at the traits, values, and competencies of global leaders—those who had successfully lived and worked in countries other than their own. This resulted in the publication of Ed Cohen's (2007) book, *Leadership Without Borders: Success Strategies from World-Class Leaders.* The book has been integrated into curriculums at a number of universities, including Northwestern University, Nova Southeastern University, and the University of Nebraska.

Leadership development at Satyam concentrated on five primary areas: leadership immersion, global business acumen, people leadership, coaching culture, and strategic business relationships. Because most programs were far more than just classroom training, they integrated action learning and coaching. Learning consultants also spent considerable amounts of time in the field observing and giving immediate feedback, using a delivery method we call "real-time learning" (see chapter 8). To provide a world-class experience, the learning ecosystem included a solid team of professionals in the field and industry experts, as well as strong partnerships with universities and learning providers around the world.

Learning's Major Impact and Recognition

Satyam's School of Leadership was launched as part of the company's learning ecosystem to nurture the growth of global business leaders at all levels of the organization. Because it was deeply linked with value creation, leadership development had a tremendous impact on the business. It played a crucial role in developing leaders who had credibility with both customers and within their respective industries.

From 2005 to the end of 2008, Satyam more than doubled its size, expanding to more than 53,000 employees based around the world. Learning and development contributed tremendously to this rapid growth. More than 7,000 associates a year were passing through a 15-week Entry-Level Technology Program. Reducing the time to deployment resulted in more than $750,000 in additional revenue each year. The Certificate of Global Business Leadership, a virtual program in partnership with U21 Global and Harvard Business School Publishing, yielded a return on investment of $5 million. Internally skilled and qualified executive coaches resulted in $15 million in savings for the organization. The percentage of leadership positions filled internally went up to more than 60 percent, as compared with 20 percent in 2005. Documented economic benefit for the New Leaders Program added up to $1.7 million. From 2005 to 2007, turnover among new leaders dropped from 8.75 to 2.76 percent a year. Re-Skilling Services, which equipped employees with the skills to meet the changing requirements of the organization, led to a savings of $32 million. Turnover was the lowest among industry peers, declining from 20 percent in 2005 to less than 11 percent in late 2008.

Major Events

Here's a rundown of the major events in this story, year by year. In 2005,

+ Satyam decides to launch the School of Leadership.
+ Ed Cohen is hired as senior vice president for the School of Leadership.

In 2006,

+ The Leadership Development Strategy is published.
+ The SatyamWay business model is released.
+ The "Leadership Without Borders" global survey of senior executives, co-sponsored by ASTD, is initiated.
+ Construction of the School of Leadership, a 240,000-square-foot facility, begins (figure A-2).
+ The extended learning management system is launched.

Figure A-1. *Nandini Darsi Shows Ed Cohen His Book in a Store at the Kuala Lumpur Airport.* (Photograph courtesy of Ed Cohen.)

Figure A-2. *Pragnya Seth, Senior Member of the School of Leadership, Participating in the Bhoomi Puja (Ground-breaking), Seeking Mother Earth's Permission to Work on Her.* (Photograph courtesy of Ed Cohen.)

+ A partnership is formed with Booz Allen Hamilton to build the Business Challenge simulation for leaders.
+ The *Satyam Leadership Journal* is launched.
+ Satyam debuts at number 15 at the ASTD BEST Awards.

In 2007,

+ Ramalinga Raju is featured on the cover of *T+D* magazine.
+ Satyam opens the School of Leadership facility.
+ Satyam hosts the Indian Society for Training & Development's national conference.
+ Satyam is ranked number 1 at the ASTD BEST Awards.
+ Satyam debuts at number 15 in the Training Top 125.
+ The real-time learning strategy is implemented.
+ The "Not for Women Leaders Only" conference is launched.

In 2008,

+ Satyam designates Ed Cohen as its first chief learning officer.
+ The Learning Center and School of Leadership merge.
+ The Business Challenge goes global.
+ Satyam climbs to number 11 in the Training Top 125.
+ Joshua Craver is named to *Training* magazine's Top Young Trainer list (figure A-3).
+ Ed Cohen wins the HR Leadership Award at the Employer Branding Institute's Third Employer Branding Awards.
+ Priscilla Nelson is given the IT People Women Leadership Award and WILL Recognition Award (WILL Women's Choice category).
+ Planet Satyam launches Asia's first web television and radio channel dedicated to learning.
+ Satyam receives seven awards from the Employee Involvement Association, six in communication excellence, and Priscilla Nelson wins the Advocate of the Year (Diversity Management-Women in Leadership) Award.
+ Ed Cohen wins the Gold in the Vanguard Category at the Fall 2008 CLO Symposium.

Figure A-3. *Joshua Craver Is Named a Top Young Trainer by* Training *Magazine.* (From *Training* magazine, May 2009.)

Figure A-4. *The School of Leadership.* (Photograph courtesy of Ed Cohen.)

In 2009,

+ Ramalinga Raju, Satyam's founder and chairman, confesses to fraud and resigns.
+ Satyam Learning World initiates the "Lights On" learning strategy.
+ Planet Satyam begins 24/7 programming.
+ Coaching for all leaders becomes required.
+ Satyam receives awards in strategic alignment, leadership development, and marketing at the Corporate University Xchange and *Fortune* magazine's 10th Annual Awards for Excellence and Innovation.
+ Satyam climbs to number 8 in the Training Top 125.
+ The learning strategy for leaders in crisis is implemented.
+ Extensive learning opportunities are provided for Satyam's displaced employees to assist them in finding new positions.
+ Satyam receives ASTD's Excellence in Practice Award for Re-Skilling Learning Services and five citations for other key offerings.

Learning at Satyam was considered to be a solid strategic investment. The transformational years of Satyam—epitomized by the School of Leadership (figure A-4)—were made possible by a solid learning ecosystem that enjoyed support from the top because learning started at the top—or so we thought. We had no idea that it would all be gone in the blink of the tiger's eye.

Appendix B:
Echoes of Innocence—
More Voices from Satyam

Throughout this book, we have shared many of the voices of those affected by the crisis at Satyam Computer Services. Here, we share more of these stories, in the hopes that they will give you a greater understanding of the impact of the crisis and the responses of the people who were associated with Satyam.

Ed Cohen
Chief Learning Officer

I decided to completely take the night off, which included not answering the phone. I remember declaring to my guests, Josh, Kate, Elana, and Howard, that I was "off duty" for the night—anything that might happen could wait until tomorrow. They laughed knowing me and how challenging this would be. They even took a few side bets on how long I could hold out. Of course this motivated me even more to take the night off. As my colleagues in India started their day, the phone began to ring. I ignored it, and everyone laughed at my ability to resist the temptation. Josh pointed out there were a lot of missed calls—32 to be exact. When the phone rang for the 33rd time, I broke down and answered it. It was Priscilla. "It's all over the news. Ramalinga Raju has confessed to overstating the revenues of Satyam since 2001. We are watching it on the news right now." Priscilla told me, "Everyone is in shock; no one knows what to do. The stock price is diving. Everyone is scared." I had no words. I needed a few moments to let the news sink in.

We turned on the television and flipped the channels from one to another to see if the news in America was reporting anything. There was nothing. I logged into email and found hundreds of messages from people who were panicking. Searching the Internet for information uncovered thousands of posts even though the announcement had come less than an hour before. So now what? We were faced with a crisis, of a magnitude far greater than anything I had ever experienced, and I was 10,000 miles away from the epicenter with little information.

With the help of my assistant, Vijay Gupta, less than an hour after the first break of the news, the associates of Satyam Learning World were participating in a live web-meeting and audio conference. What would we say to the team? How would we calm their fears? This is where having Howard Richmond, MD, around truly helped. Howard is a psychiatrist who blends humor with therapy and has an uncanny ability to bring calm to chaos. He's also our cousin. Howard wrote and flashed notes to guide me through much of the conversation. One such note truly had a profound impact on me and everyone else. "Don't let the news of today undo the successes of yesterday or tomorrow." Without realizing it, I had begun thinking that the past years spent in India working for Satyam were wasted. His short message restored my sense of being, of value, and of accomplishment. So, when we spoke to the Satyam Learning World associates, I delivered that same message. There was comfort in the thought. And, that would have to sustain us until more information came available.

Rahul Andrews
Leader, School of Leadership

It took a long time for me to find learning and development as my true calling in life. I had worked on client projects for a few years after joining Satyam. Then, in 2006, I attended a leadership program, Executive Presence, facilitated by Priscilla Nelson and Vikram Bector. Afterward, I wondered, "Who are these wonderful facilitators, where are they from, and how can I become one of them?" One conversation after another resulted in my applying for a position and making it! I had the opportunity to be what I wanted to be—a facilitator of business and people leadership programs, a coach, and a performance consultant. I was among those enabling learning as a business differentiator. I almost never took sick leave, which was an indication of the high engagement level and motivation that existed. By the end of 2008, we had reached a point of inflection, acknowledged by international accolades and laurels, poised for continuing best practices in learning.

That's when the rug was pulled out from underneath us all. We felt forced to heal rapidly so we could help others to heal. The crisis initially numbed communications across the organization, much like a headless creature rooted to its spot, not knowing where to turn next. We stepped in, communicating and acknowledging the emotions that most leaders and associates were unable to address. This crisis, unprecedented in corporate India, was not a situation any of us were equipped to handle. It finally did something to me. I broke down and wept; not once, but several times. Sometimes, these were not confined to a private space. I was invited to present at an e-learning conference in Mumbai in late January. There, I proudly shared how our learning infrastructure was creatively and cleverly leveraged to communicate across the organization during crisis. Tears welled up in my eyes as I shared through a live webcast featuring learning peers. Most tears were for what should have been. "You were too fast to live, too young to die, bye-bye, . . ."—the lyrics from the song "James Dean" sung by the Eagles continuously playing over and over in my mind.

Crisis led to fiscal resuscitation, inadvertently disrupting the spirit that had been nurtured for a long time. Faced with necessary fiscal measures instituted to prune organizational costs, I pragmatically decided to look for alternate roles outside the organization. It felt as though I had aged rapidly, experiencing several years of stress in just three turbulent months.

I took up a role heading the outsourcing research practice of a business research firm based in Pune, India. I had moved on, denizen of a learning organization that spanned cultures and spawned a new one, my desire to create an alternate future for myself and others. However, it was difficult dealing with the internal residual stress, the feelings of loss and betrayal. Six months later, I left the position deciding to take a break and catch up with life and heal any untended wounds.

Anil Santhapuri
Mentoring Program Manager, School of Leadership

The camera zoomed in. The journalist from a prominent national news channel pointed the microphone at me and said, "Hyderabad has been a place where Ramalinga Raju has been extremely popular, not just here but globally as a leader. What is the challenge that you face as a person and as a Satyam employee right now?"

I had joined Satyam in 2003 as a technical consultant. Four years later, I transferred to the School of Leadership. What I wanted to say was: "Satyam, which literally translates to truth, was shrouded in shadows of lies. My loyalty, my pride as a Hyderabadi, and my motivation was shaken and shattered." My voice trembling I responded, "Hyderabad, India has very few global companies, one of which is Satyam. As a Hyderabadi, I am proud of what Satyam has accomplished. We are going through lots of emotions personally as well as professionally. Shock, anger, and denial are just a few. This is a time to reach out and help others; that's what we're doing."

While much of the Western world had seen its share of corporate crises, in India this was unprecedented. As a first response, I was assigned to research corporate turnaround case studies. Using our web television capability, we launched a 45-minute talk show called *The Rise of the Phoenix*, wherein we discussed lessons learned from companies that had survived crisis.

It was obvious that there would be a layoff. Surviving the layoff turned into each person's mission. Those of us who did not lose their jobs coped with the loss of peers and worried about their futures.

My personal faith in humanity was shaken. The stress we experienced turned to fatigue—mental, physical, and emotional. To aid this, a few months into the crisis, a small group of us embarked on a five-day visit to an ashram in Coimbatore. The yoga, meditation, and companionship provided temporary relief. Following this, I attended a 10-day silent retreat called Vipassana. Experiencing these ancient rituals helped me put things into perspective. Still, I fluctuated between discomfort and discovery—sometimes nostalgic of the past, still cautious of the future, my wounds slowly healing. As I walk into the unknown future, the words

Figure B-1. *The Labyrinth in the School of Leadership, Hyderabad.* (Photograph courtesy of Ed Cohen.)

of Robert Frost echo in my heart and soul; "The woods are lovely, dark and deep. But I have promises to keep, and miles to go before I sleep."

Archana Vyasam
Founder, Manjeeram Academy of Fine Arts

For two years, the learning leaders at Satyam invited me to bring an Indian art form into the realm of leadership. This experience will be with me for life. Leadership in Dance graduated to its present content with much involvement from all who witnessed it. It was a perfect collaborative experience. I don't think I have come across such a work culture that included an outsider so meaningfully into theirs with such ease.

I learned a lot and was positively challenged. I had become a perfect team player without even realizing it; how beautiful. Even during the difficult times, everyone handled themselves with dignity.

(Archana Vyasam and her team contributed to leadership development through her creation, "Leadership in Dance," a presentation/performance comparing the competencies of dancers to competencies of leaders. She can be reached at the Manjeeram Academy of Fine Arts, manjeeram.com.)

Bhaskar Natarajan
Performance Consultant

We all rushed to the conference room where there was a television. To my utter shock and disbelief, the story slowly unfolded in front of us. The stock price dropped quickly—in minutes, the price nearly halved. Even then the entire story hadn't sunk in. I immediately called my wife to update her and told her not to panic. After a meeting called by the leaders, we dispersed only to gather back in small groups to further carry out our discussions.

Quickly, we jumped into action: studying models of change; creating videos, audio files, and presentations; and building activities to enhance awareness. We were part of everyone's circle of trust, so our phones were ringing constantly with people trying to find out what was happening. They were anxious about their future and wanted every bit of information we had. We told them what we knew, listened, and gave advice. We communicated openly as we implemented rapid solutions to support the wounded.

I was so affected by what happened that only, almost a year later, can I post these thoughts. Only now do I feel in control of the situation rather than the other way around. I'm proud that we weren't mute spectators or passive bystanders of tragedy. We were active partners in organizational renewal.

Chrysosthenis Taslis
Program Manager, School of Leadership

When the Satyam opportunity came about through AIESEC (a student-run, nonprofit global association), I convinced my strongly opposing family to allow me to leave our home in Greece to venture to India. Going to India would provide the opportunity to learn the culture as well as global business and international trade. My adventurous spirit was convinced.

The realities faced on arrival to Hyderabad in January 2008 weren't far from expected. I was prepared for the rough side of India (heavy pollution, traffic, endless bureaucracy, frequent power cuts, damaged road network, and so on). I was delighted to find that Satyam had robust learning and development and a leadership school run by globally known learning professionals. I joined as a learning services specialist and for a year everything was great; I was realizing my Indian dream.

It was noon and I had just come out of a meeting. No one was there. We looked around puzzled. We walked to the other wing of the building and saw the same scene: empty offices and vacant corridors. We found everyone in the labyrinth, an open amphitheater at the center of the building (figure B-1). My colleague, Rohan, bent over discreetly and whispered in my ear: "Raju confessed to cooking the books."

An avalanche of revelations; everyone, even the most senior leaders were shocked. It took a long time to realize the implications of the events. I had never seen colleagues looking so desperate. Friends and relatives called to check on me as if an earthquake had occurred. My initial shock shifted to anger. We had been cheated. To the outside world, we were all suspects. The media referred to it as the "Satyam scam." Within days, many quit and others started to look for new jobs. People were looking for something to hold onto as the trust pillars collapsed. Nothing would be the same again.

Statements of support from other firms and the government helped our wounded hearts. We leaned on our support network of family and trusted friends. At work, leaders started picking up the shattered pieces, helping others to stand up, and hoping the company would rise from its ashes. I was inspired by their efforts. In June 2009, as my visa approached expiry, I departed India leaving behind dear friends to deal with their own fate. Living in India was incredible and life-changing. I learned so much about business and life. The Satyam saga is certainly going to be studied for a long time. As a firsthand witness, I wonder if the corporate world will have the courage and discipline to learn from Satyam and avoid similar mistakes?

Nishi Levitt
Senior Leader, School of Leadership

Rush hour traffic, early morning office goers, laptops strung across their shoulders, newspaper in one hand and a large coffee mug in the other. Each morning brought newness for me. This day was no different as I entered the local coffee shop brimming with freshly baked goods. My thoughts were random. My move to America in 1990 brought on new and exciting opportunities. Then, I was single, 25 years old, and figuring out my journey in life. I was accustomed to moving across continents. There was a time when I thought "continent" was a country. Of Indian decent, I had grown up in Ireland. My father hailed from South Africa, his grandfather having come from Agra, India. My mother was a Guyanese Indian. They were an interesting mix. Neither had visited India nor were they ever educated on the Indian customs and traditions. They each retained the minimum they learned from their respective countries. Not much of their background was applicable in the Irish Catholic community of Dublin, where I was born and raised. Perhaps the background in *Leadership Without Borders* (Cohen 2007) best sums up my often confusing heritage.

Hot coffee, blaring loud music, and flies diving in and out of sparsely laid out bakery goods, and five people to help serve one person. After three and a half years, while surprises still arose, this was all a part of living in Hyderabad with my husband and young son.

We had relocated from Virginia sight unseen in 2006 for what promised to be an exciting, diverse, and cultural eye-opening opportunity to work for Satyam Computer Services. Having worked with Ed Cohen for the seven years prior, it was the instinctive trust factor that allowed our decision to move 10,000 miles away to join him in India. My senior role and position within the School of Leadership had been inching up to new heights. I was at my prime and peak of development as a leader, positioning myself, with untapped potential and a zest for creating and building networks. I delighted in growing my team and thrived on the innovation. I hobnobbed with our founder and chairman on a monthly basis at all our leadership training. I constantly reinforced his thoughts and prevalent messages to our new leaders. I believed in him, and we had a well-established rapport over many months. It felt like riding high on a wave of continued success.

How ironic that "trust" became the epitome of my life as well as the 53,000 employees around me and their families. In one fell swoop, it was all over! We were all cheated by a darkened individual who dashed all our hopes. My initial tears of disbelief melded into welts of anger. What now? Where to? I didn't realize I too was now riding the tiger. As I write this, the resilience I thought I had built up crumbles. We weren't done yet!

David Levitt
Senior Business Leader

The U.S. economy was roaring in May 2006. Our Northern Virginia home's value had more than doubled during this magical time. Both of us were willing to face some risk, so we decided to join Satyam and relocate to India. For me, the benefit was applying my experience in infrastructure services while learning about working and doing business in outsourcing. We enjoyed many new opportunities and made many contributions.

Just 30 months later, my wife, Nishi, and I watched the television as the news reported that Ramalinga Raju had been arrested. The company that employed both of us was crumbling, leaving us to pick up the pieces of our lives. We faced the uncertainty of having to head back to the states where the economy was now in shambles and jobs would be difficult to come by. We were clearly heading down a slippery slope.

Nishi and I are pragmatists at heart, so we continued to contribute and support those who worked with us. We worked to retain people. We said goodbye to those leaving, who took with them their experiences and camaraderie, a highly valued part of our business.

I learned an important component of the Indian context with the understanding of how strongly people identify with their company and its "promoter." Many could not separate the scandal from their own careers or their own self-worth. They were truly devastated and had nowhere to turn. I encouraged them to separate themselves from the debacle and to build a greater sense of their own individuality.

As the decade came to a close, I continued with the company under its new ownership. Our world has completely changed in ways we never anticipated.

Joydeb Pal
Artist in Residence

I was born on June 11, 1986, in a remote area in West Bengal State in India. My father was employed at the State Bank of India as a cashier, and my mother was a housewife. I have one elder sister. After taking voluntary retirement in 2001, my father started a jute business and lost most of our money, and our family fell into big trouble. I traveled to Hyderabad in 2006 to find work to help my family survive. I got a job in a security agency. They paid me 2,100 rupees a month ($40). That amount was not sufficient for my accommodation or to send my family. I worked 16 or 17 hours a day to earn extra money. After six months, I left that job and got another job in another security agency where I was getting 5,500 rupees a month ($110) but did not stop extra duty. My assignment was in the lobby of a Satyam building.

With that extra money, I sent some home and bought supplies for painting. I had started painting when I was seven, so whenever there was time, I painted. In 2008, I married the woman whom I had loved. Toward the end of 2008, I met with a person named Satya Somalanka Kamesh, who enjoyed my artwork. He introduced me to the leaders at School of Leadership, and the next thing I knew, my job had changed. I was now the resident artist. When Satyam got in trouble, everything fell apart. I am fine, though, because I am now a full-time artist.

Figures B-2 and B-3. (Courtesy of Joydeb Pal.)

Nicola Klein
Senior Facilitator

I was in Germany visiting family and awaiting my visa to return to India. When I went to the Indian Consulate in Cologne, the representative asked, "Satyam, really?" I had just handed him my invitation letter to get my visa. I wasn't quite sure what to say and just nodded. He said, "Not so good right now!" I nodded again. "But don't worry, . . . they will make it somehow," he finished. That gave me a lot of hope.

In late 2007, I had left my position at Booz Allen Hamilton and moved to India. I joined Ed Cohen, Joshua Craver, and Nishi Levitt, all former colleagues at Booz Allen, on their mission to build world-class learning. Now, I was on my way back to India, not knowing what I would find in the wake of the crisis. What I found surprised me. Everyone had sprung into action. It was the most amazing experience in my life. We conducted workshops across the company to help people express their thoughts and feelings. During these workshops, we asked; "What are your ideas for helping to save Satyam?" It was amazing to see the growth in people and the team spirit that brought us together every single day.

Over time, we watched as the company returned the barista coffee machines and ran out of comforts including paper towels, flipchart paper, Post-it notes, markers, paper, and ink for the printers. These annoyances proved to be small compared with the magnitude of the feelings when people started being asked to leave the company. It was like being on a rescue mission, to save as many as we could, to help them endure the pain and express themselves. We listened to their concerns and we were always available as coaches and as fellow human beings suffering the same journey.

One of my greatest lessons was, "If you have a great team of people, working together, who are passionately involved, you can make miracles happen." Having people work efficiently as a team is not easy. It takes a great deal of leadership. When I think of this amazing team, I know that "nobody wins unless everyone wins!" And we all "won" by going through this together.

Pragnya Seth
Senior Performance Consultant

After working, along with my colleague, Joshua Craver, onsite for one of our customers in North America for a week in November 2008, I said to him, "This will be the last time we will be working together." Where did that come from? I guess that is the intuition in me that has been getting sharper over time.

The economic downturn coupled with the Satyam events changed everything for me individually and for us collectively. I had a career plan, and this was not part of it. Everyone was speculating about what would remain of our company and our learning world team. Our jobs and our customers were being discussed in every corner of the building. Time went by, there were layoffs, and many others left the company to pursue safe haven.

Ten months later, in November 2009, as Priscilla Nelson and I were presenting "Learning Strategies during Turbulent Times" at the International Leadership Association Conference in Prague, I realized that my wounds had still not healed. They were still raw and sore. There are still thousands upon thousands like me who feel this terrible pain.

Kishore Goud
Graphic Designer

At 26 years old, I felt that I had achieved something big by securing a job at one of the most prestigious multinational companies in the world. I was proud to be part of such an organization and planned to have a long career there.

On that fateful day, I was working at my desk when a colleague called with the news. I was shocked, and questions buzzed in my head demanding answers. I was trying to comprehend the magnitude of the crisis and its impact on us—the employees. I reasoned that a company with 50,000 employees could not shut down shop. Many of my friends reached out to me about the news, and some friends called up to ask: "Satyam's stocks have taken a hit, do you suggest buy some stocks?" I couldn't believe how some people didn't consider our plight and looked only for their gain. My eyes opened to the game of business and the two key words "profit" and "loss." That was the reality of it.

Each cooked up his or her interpretation—the pessimist advised us to start looking for a new job; the optimists were sure that we would be retained as were a "high-performance" team. That reminded me of my mother's words, "Different tongues have different tastes."

While the storm raged on my professional front, another even more devastating storm hit my personal life. My mother fell critically ill and was hospitalized. All my efforts went into ensuring she regained her heath—all the time worried about mounting medical bills. Will I still have my job? Will the corporate medical insurance cover my mother's treatment? A few weeks later my mother expired, passing quietly in her sleep.

I joined another organization in November 2009. Even today the crisis haunts me.

Joshua Craver
Senior Performance Consultant

The day after the 2006 ASTD International Conference & Exposition ended, I flew with Ed Cohen and Priscilla Nelson to Hyderabad. This was the beginning of my new professional chapter. Having worked with Ed for five years at Booz Allen Hamilton, I had full trust we would be successful in building world-class leaders at Satyam. For the next 30 months, I lived in India while we worked tirelessly to create what became an internationally acclaimed, award-winning corporate university.

Martin Luther King Jr. said, "The ultimate measure of a man is not where he stands in moments of comfort and convenience, but where he stands at times of challenge and controversy." In early January 2009, I went to San Diego to spend some time visiting Ed. One evening, I vividly remember gazing out at the Pacific Ocean. The moon was bright, stars sprinkled the sky, and the ocean was calm. A sense of peace washed over me. The last two and a half years we had exceeded even our own expectations. All of that dissolved a few hours later, when we learned of Raju's confession. The next eight hours were intense. There was constant communication between Ed, the leadership of Satyam, and our learning and development team. The following day Ed drove me to the airport. He still hadn't slept, a testament to his leadership. We both knew there would be more sleepless nights to come. I walked through the San Diego airport and glanced over at a newsstand. The *Wall Street Journal* headline shared the news: "Corporate Scandal Shakes India, Chairman of Outsourcing Giant Resigns, Saying He Concocted Financial Result." Was this really happening?

When a crisis of this magnitude strikes no one expects it. It wounded thousands of people. As learning and development professionals, we learned how to support an organization in crisis and are better prepared for future challenges. As a team, we were respected as a true business partner that was mission critical, something for which all learning teams strive.

It was the kind of call that any leader dreads. With a heavy heart, Ed informed me that my tenure with the organization was soon to be over. This news was difficult to digest. For three years, I had dedicated my life to building leadership, and now it was over. It was the lowest point of my professional life.

Fast forward six months later: My journey to India opened the door for a new role in Mexico City working for HSBC.

Sirisha Kommireddi
Learning Services Specialist

Our little angel, Nivrithi, was born on June 5, 2008. Now we were blessed with a daughter along with an adorable son, Nihith, who was five. When she was four months, doctors diagnosed her with a condition called "biliary atresia," a congenital liver disorder that needed immediate surgery to repair the bile flow. With surgery performed in September, she was on the road to recovery, and we hoped our problems had come to an end.

Our world came shattering down in January 2009, when Ramalinga Raju's resignation resulted in utter chaos in our world again. My husband and I worked at Satyam. Our futures were at stake, disbelief, uncertainty, and insecurity became a way of life for us and for our dear colleagues.

We received another blow in February. The doctor treating our daughter confirmed the only possible permanent solution for her condition would be a liver transplant. Abnormal levels of liver enzymes were hemorrhaging the liver, and it could only be cured with a new one. On top of everything else, we needed to seek a liver donor, process formalities with the authorities, attend appointments with the transplant surgeon, and endure a long waiting period, not to mention the financial strain.

We still had no idea what was going to happen to our jobs. All this had left us shattered. Trauma and agony weighed us down. During this time, the thoughts and prayers of our friends and family comforted us and lessened the mental trauma we are going through both personally and officially. Putting it all in perspective, for some of us, the Satyam crisis was not the worst thing that could happen in one's life.

Sita Pallacholla
Program Manager

I had heard of "the bubble bursting," yet never in my most troubled dreams would I have imagined being inside that bubble. Here I was in my first job ever, and I couldn't have been happier! I will always remember my first interviews. Nervously, I sailed through one interview after the other. Everyone was warm, friendly, and happy to be there. I thought corporate was. . . . Well, actually I had no idea what corporate was, but it did not include "cheerful faces." When I got this job, I felt like I was living in a fairy tale. It was a position with major responsibilities, behaviors, and expected outcomes, and I was working with a highly passionate group of professionals. I totally blossomed! I was embraced by the senior leaders, who advised and mentored me. I was rewarded and recognized for my efforts and innovations.

Then the bubble burst. My dreams shattered, and the carpet was pulled out from under my feet. I can't say I understood it all. My world and those of so many others around me were lost—wondering what happened to happily ever after.

Venkata Subender
Program Manager

I was introduced to the School of Leadership in November 2007. I attended the Indian Society of Training & Development's national conference, which was held at the Satyam School of Leadership. I was amazed to see the facility and the investment in learning and development. The next three days were amazing. I decided that I wanted to be part of this team and started learning about it—and I eventually got a job at Satyam.

My first day, I attended a program where our chairman, Ramalinga Raju, was the chief guest. There I watched him address the 60-plus people at a dinner celebrating the firm's new leaders. I was so happy to be part of this amazing team. I was briefed on my responsibilities and started working. I met each person for a one-to-one meeting (a tradition for this team). It was a different world, a total paradigm shift from my previous experience. The first three months passed quickly. Work was actually fun. Then came team day—the leaders told us that for 89 days each quarter, we worked hard for others, but on this 90th day we could celebrate and learn.

We were all zapped by the news of the crisis, and the next few months were hideous. The day I was told I was to be let go, I accepted it with honor on the outside. But deep inside, I was in agony. Even so, I held on to the hope that the company would turn around and I would be called to resume my position.

Ramesh Kuttappan
School of Leadership Facilities

In 2006, I met the people from the Satyam School of Leadership at the Hyderabad Convention Center. While their building was under construction, they held many programs at the convention center. Every time they held a program, I made sure I was assigned as their server. I came to know all the details about each person—what they liked to eat, to drink, and how they wanted the room set up. They treated me with total respect, more than I had ever experienced. When the School of Leadership building opened, they offered me a job supervising the facility. It was then that I decided my personal dream was to become a leader of great impact. I wanted to be like the people with whom I was working.

This job was something far beyond anything I had ever imagined doing. Then the crisis came and tried to steal my dreams.

All this affected my personal life, too. My family had chosen a woman for me to marry, and her family had agreed to the match. But after the crisis hit, her family changed their minds. They were unsure of my job security. Through this tough period, it became easy to figure out who were my real friends. A small number of us became very close, and we called ourselves the "Maktub" group (an Arabic word meaning "destiny"). Sometimes I think of "going back" to where I was before Satyam, when I was a server. That's when my inner voice takes over: "Don't go back. Go forward. Be a leader."

Meet Prashanth

There are more than 11 million abandoned and orphaned children in India. Most grow up on the streets becoming beggars, drug addicts, prostitutes, or worse. Many do not survive to their 18th birthday. During our four years in India, we volunteered at a few orphanages and had the opportunity to meet many children.

Prashanth was one of more than 100 children at one of the orphanages where we volunteered (figure B-4). We were told he was an orphan. But later, we discovered that he has a mother, a sister, an auntie, and a grandmother. So how did this little boy come to live in this place?

Figure B-4. *Visiting with Prashanth.* (Photography courtesy of Ed Cohen.)

Whenever we visited, Prashanth was excited and happy to see us. He spoke in Hindi, Marathi, and Telugu but not English. He did not have use of the first two fingers on his right hand. They had been burned when he was younger. Without treatment, they had folded over and fused, rendering them unusable. We took him to meet Dr. Swain, a surgeon at Apollo Hospital, and he invited us to have Prashanth participate in a plastic surgery camp.

During the two-hour surgery, the doctors removed his scars, grafted on new skin, and straightened his fingers by placing a pin in one and a splint on the other. Due to the lack of sanitation at the orphanage, Prashanth spent most of his recovery time with us. Six weeks after the surgery, the pin and splint were removed. When Dr. Swain asked Prashanth to move his fingers, he slowly and tentatively moved them. He smiled from ear to ear and said, "Thank you for my fingers."

Prashanth is now 11. He no longer lives in an orphanage. We are sponsoring him at Sree Rajdhani Residential School in Hyderabad. The school is an oasis from the busy city. Inside, the teachers provide an excellent education. The children are taught to speak and read English, Telugu, and Hindi. They are immersed in all the wonderful traditions of India. They study, practice yoga, take time to play, and spend time in prayer.

When Prashanth is on vacation from the school, he visits his mom and sister. As we are writing his story in November 2009, Prashanth is sitting only a table away, his books open, studying. His confidence is growing as fast as he is.

John Kennedy Lives in Hyderabad

We were without a driver, not an enviable position to be in densely populated Hyderabad, where motorcycles (two-wheelers, as they are called there) and cars are as abundant as the animals and people in the streets. Driving was suicidal, unless you grew up there and knew the "rules of engagement." There were laws, of course, those written down in the books, and also those "unwritten" ones that everyone followed—common laws, like, "Oh, I missed my turn back there; . . . oh well, I'll back up that 60 feet or so" or "Oops, I meant to go the other way, I'll make a U-turn."

John was introduced to us by a friend's driver. They were cousins. We found out over the course of the next three years that John had done much in his life. He'd owned a retail store, taught martial arts where he himself earned a black belt, cleaned homes, cooked, worked for a priest, had taken care of thoroughbred horses and pedigreed dogs, and done electrical and plumbing work and also a bit of woodworking. John Kennedy was also a Catholic, and had been named after the well-known U.S. president.

John was more than our driver. He joked with us and shared the history of Hyderabad and his family. He'd had some hard times yet always counted himself as lucky. A good and honest man, he protected us fiercely. There were times when I jumped out of the car to stop someone from beating up on someone smaller, or the time I witnessed an elderly man being knocked off his scooter by a car. I climbed out to help, and John stopped me from running into the middle of the street. He flagged down the driver of the car that had hit the elderly man and got the driver to take the man to the hospital. Another time, I witnessed a security guard abusing a poor street dog and jumped out to stop it. John told me, "Madam, you are going to get me into a bad fight with that need to get into the middle of things all the time."

John lived with and supported his mother and young son Peter, who attended a private Catholic school in town. Over time, we helped him purchase his own motorcycle and a house. John was also in school. He knew that one day we would return to the United States and that his position would end, and he was trying to prepare for a better job.

Jasper, our schnoodle (part schnauzer, part poodle), who came with us from the United States, became John's constant companion. He rode up front in the "friend's seat" each and every day. They were inseparable. Jasper joined the driver's group for tea in the morning, lunch, and then again for tea in the afternoon. He was one of the guys.

When the news about Satyam broke, John was scared about his job. We immediately told him that we would continue his employment for as long as we were in India, and that we would work hard to help him find another position. John Kennedy was not "just our driver"—he was a part of our family.

References

Adubato, Steve. 2008. *What Were They Thinking? Crisis Communication: The Good, the Bad, and the Totally Clueless.* New Brunswick, NJ: Rutgers University Press.

Augustine, Norman R. 2000. Managing the Crisis You Tried to Prevent. In *Harvard Business Review on Crisis Management.* Boston: Harvard Business School Press.

Balachandran, Sudhakar. 2009. The Satyam Scandal. January 7. www.forbes.com/2009/01/07/satyam-raju-governance-oped-cx_sb_0107 balachandran.html

Bottger, Preston C. 2009. Investment in Human Capital during the Crisis: The Keys to Coaching, Developing, Retaining, and Sustaining. IMD Switzerland, July. www.imd.ch/research/challenges/TC045-09.cfm.

Brenneman, Greg. 1998. *Right Away and All at Once: How We Saved Continental.* Boston: Harvard Business Publishing.

Brenner, Richard. 2009. Crisis Coaching. November 18. www.chacocanyon.com/crisiscoaching.shtml.

Bunting, Eve, and David Frampton. 2001. *Riding the Tiger.* New York: Clarion Books.

Chaleff, Ira. 1998. Full Participation Requires Courageous Followership. *Journal for Quality and Participation,* January. Available at www.exe-coach.com/courage.htm.

Chowdary, Vandana Jayakumar, and Nagendra V. Satyam. 2009. *Computer Services: Becoming a Global Company.* Hyderabad: IBS Case Study Development Centre.

Cohen, Ed. 2007. *Leadership Without Borders: Successful Strategies from World-Class Leaders.* Singapore: John Wiley & Sons.

Collins, Jim. 2009. *How the Mighty Fall and Why Some Companies Never Give In.* Published by the author.

Dumas, Karl. 2009. Winning Share of Heart with Your Customers: Learn SixWays.www.selfgrowth.com/articles/winning_share_of_heart_with _your_customers_learn_six_ways.html.

Galagan, Pat. 2009. Trust Fall. *T+D* 11, no. 1: 26–28.

Gerstner, Louis. 2003. *Who Says Elephants Can't Dance? How I Turned Around IBM.* New York: HarperCollins.

Gibberman, Susan. 2008. *The George Burns and Gracie Allen Show.* Museum of Broadcast Communications. www.museum.tv/archives/etv/G/ htmlG/georgeburns/gerogeburns.htm.

Gorski, Ted. 2009. Get Your Edge. www.getyouredge.com.

Heathfield, Susan M. 2008. How to Change Your Culture: Organizational Culture Change. *About.Com Guide.* humanresources.about.com/od/ organizationalculture/a/culture_create.htm.

Hill, Charles W. L., and Gareth R. Jones. 2001. *Strategic Management.* Boston: Houghton Mifflin.

Huntsman, Jon M. 2009. *Winners Never Cheat—Even in Difficult Times.* Upper Saddle River, NJ: Pearson Education.

Joseph, Lison, C.R. Sukumar, and M.C. Govardhana Rangan. 2009. Satyam Seeks Financial Advice. www.livemint.com/2009/01/22001137/ Satyam-seeks-financial-advice.html.

Kaye, Beverly, and Sharon Jordan-Evans. 2008. *Love 'Em or Lose 'Em,* 4th ed. San Francisco: Berrett-Koehler.

Khurana, R., and J Weber. 2008. *Tyco International: Corporate Governance.* Boston: Harvard Business Publishing.

Kotter, John P. 2008. *A Sense of Urgency.* Boston: Harvard Business Press.

Kübler-Ross, Elisabeth, and David Kessler. 2007. *On Grief and Grieving: Finding the Meaning of Grief through the Five Stages of Loss.* New York: Scribner.

News Now. 2009. SEBI Team in Hyderabad, Satyam Raju Untraceable. January 8. www.youtube.com/watch?v=_N6O894fuVs.

Pankaj, Mishra. 2009. The Nightmare Continues for Satyam Employees. *BusinessWeek,*January28.www.businessweek.com/globalbiz/content/ jan2009/gb20090128_634376.htm.

Phani Madhav, T., and S. Umashanker. 2004. *Managing Brand Reputation: The Case of Coke, Pepsi and Cadbury in India.* Hyderabad: ICFAI Business Case Development Centre.

PRCAI (Public Relations Consultants Association of India). 1994. Resources: Research: Case Studies. November 11. www.prcai.org/ resources/cases.asp.

Raju, Ramalinga. 2009. Text of Mr. Ramalinga Raju's Statement. *Business Line,* January 7. www.thehindubusinessline.com/businessline/ blnus/05071265.htm.

Riley, H., and T. Smith. 2003. Rudy Giuliani: The Man and His Moment. Unpublished paper, John F Kennedy School of Government, Harvard University.

Seldman, Marty, and Rick Brandon. 2004. *Survival of the Savvy: High Integrity Political Tactics for Career and Company Success.* New York: Free Press.

Sify Business. 2009. SFIO Grills Raju Brothers, Srinivas. February 14. sify.com/finance/sfio-grills-raju-brothers-srinivas-news-default-jegs Sjdibeg.html.

Solzhenitsyn, Alexander. 1978. *The Gulag Archipelago 1918–1956: An Experiment in Literary Investigation.* New York: Harper & Row.

Subramaniam, Kandula. 2010. Bringing Back Satyam: How Mahindra Is Rebooting Satyam. *Businessworld Magazine,* January 18, 30–37. www .businessworld.in/bw/2010_01_09_Bringing_Back_Satyam.html.

Timmons, Heather. 2009. Satyam Officers Had Help in Fraud, Investigators Told. *New York Times,* April 6. www.nytimes.com/2009/04/07/ business/global/07outsource.html.

Vaid, Molshree. 2006. How Cadbury's Won the Battle of Worms. December 24. www.rediff.com/money/2006/dec/24cad.htm.

Vicky. 2009. Satyam Staffer Commits Suicide in Chennai—Feared Losing Job! *Zor Se Bol,* June 18. www.zorsebol.com/latest-news/satyam -staffer-commits-suicide-in-chennai-feared-loosing-job/.

Williams, Ray. 2008. Top Dogs Are Lonely: Confessions of a CEO Coach. *National Post,* February 6. www.coachfederation.org/includes/docs/ 085TopDogsareLonelypermissiongranted.pdf.

About the Authors

Priscilla Nelson is a senior-level executive with 30 years of global best-in-class talent management experience working with *Fortune* 500 companies in human resources, strategic development, performance consulting, global diversity, and succession planning. She has received international acclaim for her work in leadership development, executive coaching, and diversity. With her unique ability to recognize the additional strengths most leaders have within them and don't know how to nurture, among the notable organizations she has helped are Glaxo SmithKline, AT&T, Rollins College, Emergent Biosolutions, Titan Corporation, the U.S. government, Mahindra Satyam, and Pfizer Pharmaceuticals. She has given presentations throughout the United States, Europe, and Asia, especially in China and India. Read more about her work at her website (nelsoncohen.com).

Ed Cohen is a talent executive who has conducted business in more than 40 countries with organizations including Booz Allen Hamilton, Mahindra Satyam, Seer Technologies, National Australia Bank, Larsen & Toubro, Farmers Insurance Group, Banco Banesto, and the World Economic Forum. He has been a featured speaker around the world—from Beijing to Chicago, from Sydney to Amsterdam. He is the only chief learning officer to have led two companies to the number one ranking in the ASTD BEST Awards—Booz Allen Hamilton and Satyam Computer

Services. He is the author of *Leadership Without Borders* (John Wiley & Sons, 2007), which received multiple international accolades, and he was a contributor to *The Next Generation of Corporate Universities* (Pfeiffer, 2007). Read more about his work at his website (nelsoncohen.com).

Index